A CITY
COMES OF
AGE

D0598621

A CITY COMES OF AGE

Chicago in the 1890s

by Susan E. Hirsch
and Robert I. Goler
With a Foreword by Sam Bass Warner, Jr.

Chicago Historical Society

The exhibition *A City Comes of Age: Chicago in the 1890s* was held at the
Chicago Historical Society from October 24, 1990 to July 14, 1991.
Published in the United States of America in 1990
by the Chicago Historical Society.
© 1990 by the Chicago Historical Society.
All rights reserved.
No part of this publication may be reproduced in any manner whatsoever
without permission in writing of the Chicago Historical Society.
Library of Congress Catalog Card Number: 90-84177
ISBN 0-913820-13-X
Director of Publications, Chicago Historical Society: Russell Lewis.
Edited by Claudia Lamm Wood, Associate Editor. Designed by Bill Van Nimwegen,
Designer. Typeset in Berkeley Old Style by Impressions, Inc.,
Madison, Wisconsin. Printed by Pride in Graphics, Chicago, Illinois.

Contents

The following individuals and institutions have
generously lent objects to this exhibition:

American Police Center & Museum
Archdiocese of Chicago, Archives and Record Center
Armstrong Bros. Tool Co.
The Art Institute of Chicago
Balzekas Museum of Lithuanian Culture
Blackberry Historical Farm-Village
Bloomingdale's
Eileen Burke
Chicago Park District
Brian Scott Donovan
Perry R. Duis
DuSable Museum of African American History, Inc.
Sara C. Eklund
Field Museum of Natural History
Fourth Presbyterian Church of Chicago
The German-American Heritage Institute
T. A. Gordon
Historic Pullman Foundation, Inc.
Holy Family Catholic Church
Irish-American Heritage Center

Kolping Society
Walter and Teresa Krutz
Andy Leo
Marshall Field's
Andy Mentzer
Metropolitan Water Reclamation District of
  Greater Chicago
Museum of Science and Industry
National Museum of Health and Medicine
The Polish Museum of America
Patrick M. Quinn
St. Malachy's Catholic Church
Schwinn History Center
Spertus Museum of Judaica
Swedish American Museum Association of Chicago
The Time Museum
Carol Turchan
University of Chicago
Vienna Sausage Manufacturing Company
Paul M. Walsdorf

A City Comes of Age: Chicago in the 1890s has been made possible
through the extraordinary generosity of:

Sara Lee Foundation
National Endowment for the Humanities, a federal agency

Additional gifts have been received from:

Lloyd A. Fry Foundation
Hal Riney & Partners, Inc.
Illinois Humanities Council and Illinois General Assembly
Mr. and Mrs. Newton N. Minow
Harris Family of Banks
MIDCON Corp
Polk Bros. Foundation
United Airlines
Waste Management, Inc.

Preface

by Susan Page Tillett

Each age writes the history of the past anew with reference to the conditions uppermost in its own time. . . . The aim of history, then, is to know the elements of the present by understanding what came into the present from the past. For the present is simply the developing past, the past the undeveloped present. . . . The antiquarian strives to bring back the past for the sake of the past; the historian strives to show the present to itself by revealing its origin from the past. The goal of the antiquarian is the dead past; the goal of the historian is the living present.

Frederick Jackson Turner, 1891

What makes history so interesting to me is that I have come to believe what Frederick Jackson Turner knew and stated so eloquently in 1891: history is not a static body of facts, but rather an ever-developing story, which changes as our relationship to the past changes. It is as much about ourselves as it is about other people and other times. The constant revision of history is not based on a belief that what was written in the past is wrong and that now we have it right, but is rather a natural process of stating our perceptions from our current vantage point.

Just as history books reveal a particular view of the past, so do museum exhibitions. At the Chicago Historical Society, a visitor can see the many different visions of Chicago history: the irresistible lure of those miniature recreations, the dioramas made in the 1930s; the living history of the Pioneer Life Gallery, created in the 1960s; and the exuberant jumble of artifacts in the more recent Chicago History Galleries, all of

In the 1890s, as today, people thronged to the Loop for shopping, business, and entertainment.

which can be seen on any visit to the Society. To these collected visions of our history we add *A City Comes of Age: Chicago in the 1890s*. This exhibition and the story behind its development tell much about the Chicago Historical Society today and its plans for the future.

The Chicago Historical Society is clearly changing the way it sees itself and presents itself to the public. A long history and a strong sense of tradition, which might have served as a rationale for a nostalgic look at bygone days, have instead formed the foundation for a vigorous process of self-examination, the development of a stronger sense of identity, and the commitment to a new mission to serve "the living present." This long-range planning culminated in the formal adoption of a new mission statement in 1989, in which the staff and the board of trustees took on the active role as "the historian of metropolitan Chicago," with a commitment to help the city's diverse audiences understand their history and what it means to their lives today and tomorrow.

When I joined the staff in 1987, the planning process that led to the new mission statement was well underway. My charge was to direct and coordinate the activities of the curators to fulfill that emerging mission. I ad-

dressed the exhibition program first, since it is the vehicle through which the largest number of people encounter our collections and interpretations of history.

Good exhibitions are the products of the whole institution, not just one curator. For that reason a committee that included senior staff in education, design, and publications as well as curators, the director of the Society, and myself, charted a comprehensive plan for exhibitions. This hard-working group deserves tremendous credit for taking on the difficult task of translating the mission into action. We were assisted in this work by two urban historians whom we asked to join us in thrashing out the best way to convey history through the combination of objects and ideas. We owe Michael H. Ebner, professor of history at Lake Forest College and Perry R. Duis, associate professor of history at University of Illinois at Chicago, tremendous gratitude for their willingness to work in partnership with us, to help us develop a model that has been acclaimed by both the academic and the museum professions.

Three major decisions emerged from those early meetings: we were committed to helping the public understand our own time through interpretation of the past, we would focus on Chicago as a city, and we would work in part-

nership with academic historians. Realizing that the end of the century and millennium were upon us, we decided to concentrate on a series of five biennial exhibitions that would begin in the fall of 1990 and continue every other year through the last year of the final decade of the twentieth century. The series, "Prologue for the New Century," will look at different aspects of the city's history over the past one hundred years and ask visitors to consider ramifications of that history for the twenty-first century. We purposely have not set the schedule for the entire series, with the hope and expectation that by leaving ourselves open to the process, new issues that we could not identify or articulate in 1987 would emerge. This identification of new issues is already happening, as we consider public housing, pollution, education, public health, and racial tension as possible topics.

For each exhibition, we will pair a curator from our staff with an outside expert who brings a new perspective and expertise. In the biennial exhibitions, we will challenge assumptions and experiment with new techniques of design and interpretation. Once we had committed ourselves to the series, we decided to start with an examination of how Chicago was formed. Although Chicago had been settled largely in the nineteenth century, its rebuilding after the Chicago Fire of 1871 combined with its strategic position as the linchpin of a national distribution system dramatically compressed its development as a city.

As an impressive number of centennials approached in the 1990s, we identified the 1890s as a critical decade in the formation of Chicago as a major metropolitan center. To help the public understand the complexities of life in the city, we considered issues that urban historians look at: Why did Chicago undergo such tremendous growth in the 1890s? Who were the people who flooded into the city from around the country and the world? What were their lives like? What were their problems and their dreams? Who had the power to decide what kind of city Chicago would become? Why were so many cultural institutions formed during this decade? What is the legacy of the 1890s for Chicago a century later? What resources do we bring to the problems facing us at the dawn of the twenty-first century?

To help us pose these questions, we sought the help of two outstanding urban historians who were interested in presenting these issues to a broad public. Since he published *Streetcar Suburbs* in 1962, Sam Bass Warner, Jr., has been regarded as a pioneer in the study of cities. The depth of

his knowledge and the breadth of his experience have been a tremendous resource. It is our good fortune that at this point in his career the idea of lending his perspective to our study of Chicago in a museum setting appealed to him. When we asked Sam to join us in developing the first biennial exhibition, he suggested a modification on the original curator and historian partnership. He proposed the addition of Susan Hirsch, assistant professor of history at Loyola University in Chicago, because of her extensive research and knowledge of Chicago during this period and her interest in public history. Members of the project staff have learned a tremendous amount about Chicago in the 1890s thanks to her willingness to share her knowledge and to her intellectual leadership.

Susan has worked very closely with co-curator Robert I. Goler, the Society's curator of decorative and industrial arts, to develop an exhibition that examines the fascinating issues of the 1890s through more than one thousand objects. Combining objects and ideas has required constant flexibility on the part of both curator and scholar, and both are to be commended for their sustained efforts.

A City Comes of Age follows *We the People* and *A House Divided* in a series of successful collabora-

tions between distinguished historians and the curators of the Chicago Historical Society. Each team has worked differently, drawing upon the combination of strengths that the partners bring to the topic or develop in the process. At our first meeting I was pleased and a little surprised to note that the historians were very conscious of the audience and had good ideas about what might capture the imaginations of the average family on a Sunday outing. Although Sam and Susan's primary job was to help us frame the exhibition in historical concepts, neither one ever lost sight of the demands of the exhibition medium. Likewise, Bob Goler and other key members of the staff used new information about Chicago in the 1890s to inform the choice of artifacts to convey the historical ideas.

This exhibition, which was originally developed by a group of staff more than three years ago, has continued to be a collaborative effort. The decision to begin with ideas and find objects to convey those ideas to the public has challenged the entire project staff to think creatively and to assume new roles, an equally exhilarating and terrifying process. Such a journey makes the project director particularly grateful for the efforts of fellow team members. In addition to the curators, who were largely responsible for the content of the show, I would like to thank Ellsworth H. Brown, president and director, for his constant challenge to make history useful; Marc Hilton, vice president of development, for his early ideas and enthusiasm for the topic; Russell Lewis, director of publications, and Lizabeth Cohen, assistant professor of history at Carnegie Mellon University, for their good counsel through the three-year process; Andrew Leo, director of design, and his staff, Michael Biddle, Bill Van Nimwegen, Wally Reinhardt, Virginia Heaven, and Ted Gibbs for their willingness to work closely and creatively with the curators to realize the exhibition concepts; Claudia Lamm Wood, associate editor, Patricia Bereck Weikersheimer, assistant editor, and Jennifer Schima, publications intern, for focusing and communicating the ideas through labels and the accompanying publications; Amina Dickerson, director of education and public programs, and associate educators Eva Olson and Lynn McRainey for bringing the 1890s to life through their imaginative programming; Mary Janzen, assistant to the president, for her dual role as author of the successful National Endowment for the Humanities grant and producer of the audiovisual components; and Kim Kane for serving as the faithful research

assistant, tracking down literally thousands of facts and images.

I owe special thanks to the members of the curatorial staff who willingly joined the project team to add their own expertise and suggestions—Libby Mahoney, Diane Ryan, Ralph Pugh, Susan Samek, and Wendy Greenhouse. Thanks also to Larry Viskochil, Janice McNeill, Emily Clark, Cathy Olson, Laura Montgomery, Archie Motley, Linda Evans, and Corey Seeman for making collections available. Tim Hagan, assistant registrar, Mike Ryan, collections manager, and their crew did an outstanding job of gathering and keeping track of the many artifacts. Conservators Carol Turchan, Anna Kolata, Nancy Rubin, and Jeanne Mandel worked their magic on one-hundred-year-old pieces. Photographers John Alderson and Jay Crawford photographed the artifacts with their customary professionalism and good cheer. Lorraine Mason, curatorial secretary, typed and retyped the countless lists, labels, and schedules and generally kept us organized.

Marc Hilton, Beth Dunworth, and Barbara Reed of the development staff have been supportive of the project since the beginning and ran a very successful fund-raising campaign. Each of our donors—federal, foundation, corporate, and individual—has been

very involved in and committed to this project. Special thanks go to Ben Rothblatt and the Lloyd A. Fry Foundation, which Mr. Rothblatt directs, for their successive planning and implementation grants. The National Endowment for the Humanities has once again provided support, awarding us our third major exhibition grant in three years, thereby allowing us to realize our long-range goals by building on our cumulative experience. The exhibition's major corporate underwriter is the Sara Lee Foundation. We are deeply grateful for the early support and encouragement of the foundation's executive director, Gretchen Miller Reimel, and the corporation's chairman, John H. Bryan, Jr. It is also a pleasure to acknowledge the additional support (as of this writing) from the Harris Family of Banks, the Illinois Humanities Council, and Waste Management, Inc. Mr. and Mrs. Newton N. Minow's contribution is particularly touching to the staff of whom they are so regularly supportive. Pat Kremer, Linda Bricker, and the public relations staff have outdone themselves once again by joining their talents with those of Hal Riney & Partners to promote the exhibition.

While the list of museum staff to whom we feel gratitude is virtually as long as the list of people working at the Society since the exhibition demanded time, energy, and talents from almost the entire staff, the list outside the institution may be even longer. One of the great revelations of the exhibition process was that we didn't have much of the material that we needed. Dozens of phone calls ultimately lead to hundreds of contacts and a series of meetings, adventures, and loans that have greatly enhanced the exhibition and established important new relationships for the Chicago Historical Society. I particularly enjoyed my own experiences with the ethnic museums and community organizations, which made the city come to life for me in countless new ways. For their generosity in sharing their stories, history, and treasured artifacts with us, our heartfelt thanks to Robert E. Armstrong, Patricia H. Atwood, Mary Ann Bamberger, C.W. Baxa, Carolyn Blackman, Louise Blackman, Marlena Blumerska, Peggy Bradley, Michael Brown, Richard Bumstead, Teresa Campbell, Christine Chakoian, Mel Clark, Nina Cummings, Mary Cygan, Brian Donovan, Perry R. Duis, Sara C. Ecklund, Susan Eleuterio, Keith Gill, Thomas Gora, Frank Guercio, Philip Harris, Mary Hild, Harry Hooper, James Hurd, Kathy Hussey-Arntson, Carol Ideler, Kineret Jaffe, Mary Ann Johnson, Christopher Kamyszew, Elizabeth Kaye, Frank Kilkes, Janice Klein, Donald Kloster, Teresa Krutz, Mary Kuzniar, Kerstan Lane, Katherine Lee, Delores Loeber, Margot McMahon, Michele Madison, Grace Mason, Edith Mayo, Daniel Meyer, Peggy Montes, Constance Mortell, Brenda Nelson-Strauss, Father Thomas O'Gorman, Mary O'Reilly, Useni Eugene Perkins, Geoffrey Plantin, Richard Popp, Ramon Price, Val Ramonis, Randall A. Reinisch, John Rybski, Joseph Saccomonto, Chuck Sadowski, Pauline Saliga, Deborah Sanders, Reverend David Saunders, Robert Sengstacke, John Shallcross, Homer Sharp, Marion Shepherd, Ellen Skerrett, Tim Slavin, John Smith, Bill and Mary Solt, Robert Soudek, Jack Sowchin, Edward Stratman, Marcia Szpak, Raymond Tindale, Will Tippens, Sue Topp, Jack Trainer, Paul Walsdorf, Ian Wardropper, Olga Weiss, Muriel Wilson, Martha Wolff, and Susan Yerkes.

The process of assembling this exhibition has challenged this staff to reconsider our relationship to the past, to the future, and to Chicago. We hope it will do the same for you.

Foreword

by Sam Bass Warner, Jr.

This exhibition invites you to explore Chicago of the 1890s. In doing so you may refashion your knowledge and assumptions and reinterpret your traditions to form a civic consciousness that will help you envision a better life for yourself and your city.

The civic heritage of Chicago, like the traditions of other American cities, is framed in the ever-popular stories of the grandparents that every family cherishes, stories of the struggles and successes of those who came before us. Our grandparents' stories constitute the central civic myths of Chicago. These personal narratives, when summed, tell of the houses, the factories, the skyscrapers, the stockyards, the warehouses, and the railroads of the city. Chicago is a city the small-town boys and girls and the farmers' sons and daughters built. Yet to merely repeat the grandparents' tales, to attempt to celebrate their triumphs in 1990 as they celebrated them in 1893 would neither honor the past nor sustain its memory in the present. For civic myths to stay alive, they must be retold by the grandchildren, and their children ever after, but they must be retold in ways that fit current circumstances and current understanding.

The tensions between memory and fact are the driving force of any historical exhibition. Like all museum exhibitors we have selected objects

Just as Chicagoans of today ride public transportation to the Loop, Chicagoans of the 1890s relied on the new electric streetcar.

from the past that we think will heighten that tension and will thereby stimulate the imaginations of people. This is, however, a public exhibition, not a grandmother's attic, so we have arranged our materials carefully, combining the commonsense and scholarly meanings of objects.

What, for example, is the meaning of a bicycle? The safety bicycle, an invention of the late 1880s, required no special skill to ride and became popular in that decade. As a machine and as something made in a Chicago factory it has one meaning. As a new device that cost more than a poor family could afford it has another meaning. As an invention that women and girls, as well as men and boys, could use it has still a third meaning. And as a new mode of transportation that allowed boys and girls to escape the eyes of their families and their neighborhoods it has still a fourth meaning.

We chose to concentrate on the third and fourth meanings, the women's and young people's, because these meanings were elements in a complex of events that rapidly transformed life in Chicago in the 1890s. Scholars have labeled that vastly significant event the demographic transition; everyone knows it as the revolution in family life. It began in the 1890s and continues today.

Let this foreword provide a map for your exploration of the Chicago of the 1890s. Entering the exhibition, you are a stranger among strangers, coming to the city in a railroad car, as most Chicagoans then did. In the first exhibition area you see the jobs and the conditions of work you and your fellow immigrants share. You will see the churches and the societies of the immigrant and black neighborhoods that you would live in. The first clues to the city of the past tell you how Chicagoans settled and made their livings. Scholars arrange these clues of what made Chicago grow and what brought the immigrants to it as the study of the history of a regional economy, which links the business news and the family news.

For all the achievements of settling and building a city, Chicago in the 1890s was not a city of consensus and harmony. It was full of varied conflicts, and in 1894 it exploded with the massive national strike, the Pullman Strike. The strike revealed what scholars call a crisis in authority. In this exhibition that crisis serves as a flare to illuminate the dissatisfaction of thousands of Chicagoans from all walks of life. We describe the problems that they identified a century ago to demonstrate the patterns of their discontent and their hopes for change.

As you walk across the exhibition's electric-light bridge of the World's Columbian Exposition, you will see a dramatic expression of some of

those hopes. Chicago business leaders felt the city had not received sufficient recognition for what had been accomplished. They wanted to show off their skills and achievements, and they wanted to display their successes in the most fashionable style of their day—the architecture of imperial Paris. The fair was a Chicago triumph, and as you move through the second room of the exhibition you will find reverberations of the hopes expressed in the fair.

The miscellany of popular and well-known objects in the second room of the exhibition—the bicycle, the dress, the Sanitary Canal, the playground, and the department store—are known to us all; all survive in some form to this day. But what do they mean to us in 1990? In the conjunction of these many disparate public and private creations, schol-

Chicago of the 1890s was a city of strangers. Immigrants traveled to the city on trains, drawn by the opportunities for work and the excitement of the urban environment.

ars today find the devices that encouraged young people to try new ways of living, to break away from the cultural traditions of their parents. From these creations emerge the solutions to the problems that individuals saw in their city.

Finally, you will find some of Chicago's most distinguished institutions represented: the Chicago Symphony Orchestra, the University of Chicago, the Field Museum, Hull-House, and the Art Institute. Each has its own history, but as a group of institutions with beginnings in the 1890s, they demonstrate the effectiveness of Chicago as a place where the like-minded could gather and transform their private skills and enthusiasms into powerful and enduring public expressions.

This 1895 advertisement for the Wilson Distilling Company embodied the Chicagoan's belief that biggest meant best.

In today's urban history scholarship, we think of cities as centers of communication and exchange whose activities are nested within regional, national, and international networks. These centers communicate with one another in a hierarchical fashion: the biggest and most active world metropolises communicate outwards and downwards, to each other, and to the smaller cities. The smaller places in turn serve as centers for their regions. In the nineteenth century, Chicago and its businessmen organized the trade in lumber products from Michigan, Wisconsin, and Minnesota, and they managed the output of the mines of Illinois, Minnesota, and Colorado. They also directed the traffic in pigs, cattle, and grains for the whole Mississippi Valley. Chicago's wholesalers, bankers, and shippers also organized the supply and sales of the products of the mill towns from Rockford to Denver,

The Regional Economy

At the center of a hub of railways connecting the Mississippi Valley to the rest of the country, Chicago organized and controlled the economy of the region.

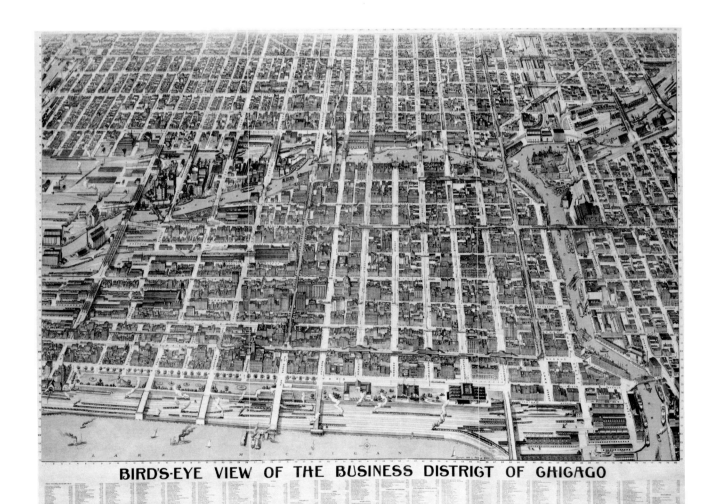

BIRD'S-EYE VIEW OF THE BUSINESS DISTRICT OF CHICAGO

while Chicago's railroads stretched south to the Gulf of Mexico and west to the Pacific.

The myriad roles in Chicago made the city the boom town it was, and from these varied roles emerged the successes told in the grandparents' tales. We have begun our exhibition with the theme of the city of a million strangers to suggest the meaning to society of the flood of people that poured into the new metropolitan center. When comparing the 1890s with the 1990s, remember that few residents had been born in Chicago and that most who knew each other had not been acquainted for long. Also remember that today Chicago is once again becoming an immigrant city, only this time with newcomers from Mexico, Central America, the Caribbean, and Asia.

Chicago still organizes the Midwest and the supply, manufacture, and sale of its myriad products and services. But it has fallen in the hierarchy of American cities from the second to the third rank because an even larger regional economy, the economy of Los Angeles and the Southwest, has come into being since the 1890s.

When considering this loss of rank, Chicagoans today might wish to reexamine the spirit of rivalry that animated the city's leaders a century ago. During the 1890s Chicagoans strove for the biggest and the best, and as they did so they often conflated the two measures. The big store, the giant factory, the tall building, the far-reaching railroad were constructed with the hope of besting New York, London, or Paris. In today's fast-changing world economy it is surely a point of prudence and security to strive always to be the best. But the shadows of the rail yards, the rusty sheds of the steel mills, and the weed-covered stockyards suggest to Chicagoans that they might be wise to let go of the city's devotion to bigness. Yet bigness there was in 1890, and bigness there still is. It appears in this exhibition in the works of George Pullman, in the department stores, and in the civic enterprise of the "Eighth Wonder of the World," the Sanitary Canal.

The Crisis in Authority

A giant regional economy with its big new corporations and its streams of incoming workers created new relationships among employers and employees that challenged the ways of both day laborers and craftsmen. In this exhibition we especially focus on the world of Chicago work because it was the promise of employment that drew thousands to the city.

Anyone in the 1890s with a new contract, a new product, or a new factory always found hands ready and able to undertake the work. The simple machines and processes of much of Chicago's industry created a

A massive civic undertaking, the Sanitary Canal opened in 1900 and was called "The Eighth Wonder of the World."

multitude of jobs for those who had only learned the skills of the farm or the small-town crafts. Although the press encouraged prejudices against foreigners and African-Americans, and many new and long-settled residents felt entitled to express their citizenship in anti-Catholic, anti-Jewish, and anti-black attacks, the newcomers were essential. Chicago could not, given the simple machinery of the era, grow and prosper without vast armies of machine tenders and laborers. Therefore, in considering the 1890s, imagine its workers as a huge reservoir, an enormous resource that could be drawn upon whenever the city needed something done or something made.

As the city grew, it added thousands of new flats and houses built by small contractors with the work of small gangs of laborers, carpenters,

THE VANGUARD OF ANARCHY.

and masons. Local stores emerged on the streets of cable car and street-car lines, and many small factories and shops employed less than two dozen workers. Such places were not without conflicts. Chicago craftsmen fought with their employers over proper use of machinery, piece rate for tasks, hours, and hirings and firings. Yet the organization of Chicago's craftsmen and workers into local unions and citywide federations was able to maintain some equitable balance between the interests of employee and employer.

The labor crisis of the 1890s arose outside these small firms and work crews. It came from the giant new enterprises, the railroads, the national manufactories, the places that hired hundreds, even thousands, of employees. The scale of business of such firms insulated them from disci-

Facing page: Fear of threats to the established order is shown in this 1894 cartoon in which labor leader Eugene V. Debs is carried, princelike, by Governor Altgeld. Below: In addition to the large firms that flourished in the 1890s, small manufacturing concerns, such as this leather goods factory, continued to prosper.

The National Guard, here ranged in front of the Arcade Building in the Pullman community, was called out by President Cleveland to end the Pullman Strike of 1894.

pline merely by the city, as the leaders of the Chicago Civic Federation learned to their surprise during the Pullman Strike of 1894.

On the big railroads and in the big factories, places like McCormick's, the employers were trying to wrest full control of the design and execution of the work away from the craftsmen and work crews they had hired. It was a long drawn-out power struggle, but one of high combat within the big firms in Chicago during the 1890s.

The concentration of labor power within these firms frightened many people. George Pullman was so frightened by the challenge to his authority that his workers presented that he refused even to speak with them. President Cleveland was so frightened when he discovered in the Pullman Strike that Chicago railroads had become a control point in the nation's economy that he called out the federal troops. Fear and denial were the responses of the leaders of Chicago in the 1890s. The builders of the city's giant enterprises refused to examine what they had wrought. They wished to continue to treat their corporations as if they were like any small business proprietorship. Crush the unions, they said. By contrast, the wealthy machine builder of Cleveland, Mark Hanna, had learned more: "A man who won't meet his own men half-way is a God-damn fool!"[1]

Modes of work have changed since the 1890s, and as a result the craftsmen and work crews have lost control over the way they perform their tasks. Today it is the self-directed professionals who are experiencing the discipline and conflicts of large organizations. Perhaps as visitors review the events of the 1890s they will consider these century-old conditions in light of the problems of today's management-controlled offices, stores, and plants.

Sometimes the most important events of history do not manifest themselves in dramatic ways, like a strike or an election, but are the products of many small events, a tangle of private and public decisions. When summed, the modest stories of the young men and women who traveled to the city, married, and raised children form one of the most significant events of the modern era, an intricate social process that scholars call the demographic transition. This transition marks a time of change from late to early marriages, from large families to small, and from the meager wealth necessary for food and shelter to a more generous standard of living that allowed millions security and play as well as survival.

The generation of the 1890s, the American farm boys and girls and the village and town youth of Europe, participated in a complex social process that revolutionized the family patterns of the modern city. As we look back, we know that the old photographs of the young people in their wedding clothes suggest a false continuity from generation to generation. The immigrants to Chicago did not merely repeat their parents' behavior, nor did their children repeat theirs.

The very living conditions of Chicago after the fire of October 9, 1871, were new. Through the complex interactions of the housing market and the institution building of the immigrants, Chicagoans established socially segregated neighborhoods, clusters where the rich lived separated from the poor, the craftsmen from the merchants, the Germans from the Swedes, and the people from the South from the people from New England. Previously cities had not been so segregated. Fueled by an abun-

The Demographic Transition

Social segregation created neighborhoods in which like immigrants gathered and English was rarely spoken. This gymnastic show and concert celebrated the laying of the cornerstone of the new Hall of Turnverein Vorwärts.

dance of cheap land and building materials, coupled with low wages, Chicago in the 1890s became the forerunner of today's segregated and sprawling city.

The booming private market in houses and flats depended on vast public works to make the neighborhoods safe for human habitation. The great public water and sewer constructions of the city reinforced the efforts of reformers to ensure that the food was clean and safe and the care of infants adequate. Together these public and private initiatives created urban environments of unprecedented safety: for the first time in Chicago's years as a big city, and for the first time in the history of all American and European large cities, it became possible during the

Reformers, such as this representative of the Infant Welfare Society, strove to ensure that food was uncontaminated and the care of infants adequate. These efforts, along with the development of a public water works system and the construction of new sewers, led to a dramatic drop in Chicago's infant mortality rate.

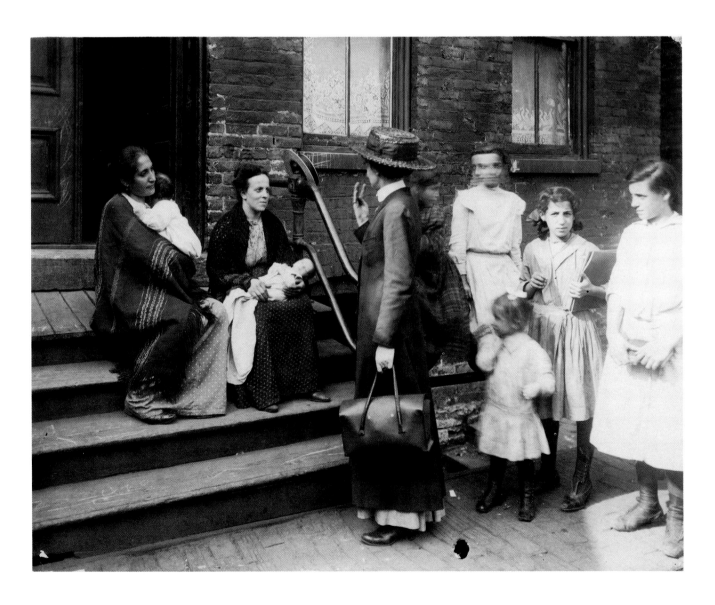

1890s for the population to grow from reproduction alone. Previously, infant mortality had been so high that the city could just maintain itself without fresh immigration. The increased possibility that children would survive seems to have influenced young people to have smaller families. Additional forces, however, encouraged limiting the size of families.

The image of life in the 1890s passed down through the grandparents' tales is one of families with many children and of settled social routines in the segregated neighborhood enclaves. Yet nothing was settled. The houses were brand new, the churches were even newer, and the fraternal organizations, athletic clubs, and union locals were new. All had been built by strangers, people who didn't know each other in the old town or the old country. And the newcomers' children didn't settle down to continue these newly established social routines. Instead they went beyond the confines of the neighborhoods to seek adventure in amusement parks, in dance halls, and in theaters. There they met new people, courted in new ways, married younger, and raised fewer children than their parents or grandparents did.

This change from the large family to the small one is a major event of twentieth-century urban societies. Along with it came the increased freedom for women and a changing culture for youth. The elements of change appear all through our exhibition, but the viewer will have to assemble the many parts to imagine being a young person in the 1890s. The relative prosperity of the world of work, the opportunity to own a house, and the new public works contributed to the change. But the new material pursuits made possible by the new stores and the new culture of youth were also essential agents in the change. This demographic transition was a momentous and exceedingly complex change that comprised millions of individual preferences; it mixed the vastness of modern engineering with the fashions of sports clothes, and it depended on such mundane activities as clean housekeeping and such basic morality as not selling spoiled meat or adulterated milk. As a generation also experiencing a revolution in family life, we have a sensitivity to these commonplace details of urban living that perhaps an audience of twenty years ago would have lacked.

The most distant aspect of the former Chicago, perhaps the most difficult atmosphere for today's visitor to recapture, is the spirit of optimism that pervaded the city. It was an outward-looking, city-oriented optimism that transcended mere confidence in personal success. The economic growth of the city cannot account for this civic energy. Indeed,

The Urban Expression of Private Passions

Right: Reformers targeted City Council's corrupt granting of trolley franchises in the 1890s.

CITY COUNCIL: "LIKE ANYTHING ELSE, MR. YERKES? IF SO, JUST ASK FOR IT."

Right: Reformers targeted City Council's corrupt granting of trolley franchises in the 1890s.

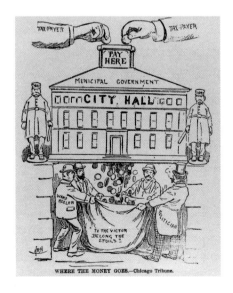

This 1894 cartoon depicts the reformers' low opinion of City Hall.

during the last decade of the nineteenth century, the city suffered the deep national depression of 1893–97, and earlier decades of prosperity had not stimulated the imaginations of Chicagoans as the nineties did.

The special quality of the 1890s flowed from the urban orientation of its local culture. Chicago's citizens during that decade acted the way citizens of successful cities always do. They expected that if they announced their personal visions in speeches in meeting halls, on street corners, or in the newspapers and books, the like-minded would hear the message and join them. Chicagoans in the 1890s believed that despite unemployment and hard times, political corruption and racial and ethnic animosities, meanness and fraud in business, a vision of a better future would find its supporters within the city, and thus individuals and small groups could improve their lives.

After all is said about the Haymarket Affair of 1886, it was not the mere preaching of revolution that frightened Chicagoans. The United States had been born in revolution a century earlier. It was the fear that their fellow Chicagoans would listen to and join the anarchists that frightened the comfortable. So too with the English journalist William Thomas Stead, who visited the city in 1893. His November 1893 lecture and his book, *If Christ Came to Chicago,* which resonated in the souls of many Chicagoans, helped to launch the Civic Federation and the movement to control the corrupt traction franchises of Charles T. Yerkes.

So it was the new cultural, educational, and social Chicago institutions whose foundings are recalled by this exhibition. Each one owes its existence to the private passion of one or a few persons. Each institution developed its enthusiasts who joined the instigators to make public what had formerly been only personal and private. Hull-House began with the explorations and convictions of Jane Addams, and it grew to be a new kind of school and neighborhood social service agency that far transcended the personal aid common in those days. Hull-House became the crossroads for immigrants and their children, experimental teachers, and social investigators and reformers. All the other great institutions of the nineties created similar crossroads and meeting places.

The Chicago Symphony Orchestra grew out of financier Charles Norman Fay's enthusiasm for classical music. The Art Institute became a major public collection because the lawyer son of a lumber merchant, Martin A. Ryerson, had a passion for painting and sculpture. He spent his lifetime studying European art and persuading people like Mrs. Potter Palmer to make private collections public. The Field Museum grew out of a passion for American Indian relics that had captured the lumberman Edward E. Ayer. The University of Chicago was born of the vision of two Chicago Baptist ministers and a Yale professor of Greek, Dr. William R. Harper. The trio envisioned a university embodying the new devotion to research, a university that could be worthy of a modern city. The enthusiasm of Reverend Frederick T. Gates, Reverend Thomas W. Goodspeed, and Professor Harper captured John D. Rockefeller's millions as well as the gifts of many wealthy Chicagoans, including an observatory from Charles T. Yerkes. The university quickly became a mecca for those who wanted to study and practice the new social sciences.

The essential element that joins these diverse organizations lies in their urban visions and urban roles. By 1890 Chicago had grown too large for the like-minded to meet on the sidewalks or in the restaurants or halls of the Loop. If the energy of fresh ideas was to be transformed into action, the city required new gathering places for strangers who shared similar visions. Five new institutions of the 1890s, Hull-House, the Chicago Symphony Orchestra, the Art Institute of Chicago, the Field Museum, and the University of Chicago all provided such settings, and it is as public meeting grounds that they flourished. Their magic derived from the personal optimism and passion of their founders who believed that in the city of Chicago one could gather like-minded strangers together, and that together they could make their city a richer and better place.

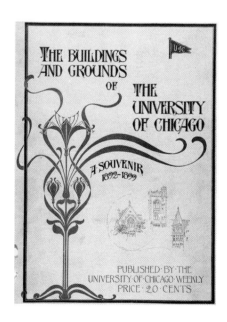

The University of Chicago was one of the many institutions founded in Chicago in the 1890s that united the enthusiasm of visionaries and reformers with the financial contributions of businessmen.

The Metropolis of the West

by Susan E. Hirsch

B y the 1890s Chicago had reached a crucial juncture. It had grown from a village to the "Metropolis of the West" with little civic unity: groups and individuals had pursued opportunities and many had prospered, but few had considered the welfare of the public as a whole. Rapid economic development and immigration had undercut any sense of community. Great inequality of wealth and a wide variety of cultures and languages characterized the city. People identified primarily with the communities they had created on the basis of shared ethnicity, race, or class. In the 1890s the costs of this fragmentation reached a new high as Chicagoans faced the challenges created by massive immigration, rapid industrialization, and unrestrained urban growth.

Chicago had grown by attracting people in search of economic opportunity and the excitement of urban life. Although the city continued to offer these inducements, many Chicagoans wanted more. They had visions of urban life that transcended what had been created in the past. In the 1890s they voiced a host of complaints about the quality of life in their city. The depression of 1893–97 with its unemployment and the massive Pullman Strike of 1894 elicited the concern that Chicago did not offer justice for workers and compassion for the poor.[1] Virtually all Chicagoans feared that the city was becoming unlivable. Severe water

Chicago's skyscrapers and busy downtown streets (facing page) symbolized the great city it had become by the 1890s. State Street north from Madison. Photograph by Barnes-Crosby.

Trumpeting its art, science, and industry, Chicago proclaimed itself the Metropolis of the West in the 1890s and sought to surpass New York as the nation's premier city. The Chicago of To-day: The Metropolis of the West, 1892. [Plate 1]

and air pollution was ruining the physical environment. Poor service and great cost plagued public services such as garbage collection and the streetcar lines.

These complaints hardly exhaust the list of problems Chicagoans identified in the 1890s. The culture of the city, that cosmopolitan life that had attracted so many, was also found wanting. Some Chicagoans deplored the lack of morality in the city with its widespread prostitution, drunkenness, and gambling. Wealthy Chicagoans who had visited the great cities of Europe and America criticized the absence of institutions of high culture in Chicago—especially those of art and music. Young Chicagoans grew restive with their parents' definitions of appropriate leisure activities and sought new forms of fun.

Despite the severe depression during the 1890s, Chicagoans felt optimistic about themselves and their futures. They had "new ideas, new ambitions and inspirations."[2] Like-minded individuals came together in private groups and created new institutions to solve the problems that concerned them. At the same time Chicagoans began in small ways to develop a growing sense of unity. They developed citywide coalitions to address some problems and sought to expand the government's responsibility for improving the city. This widespread questioning of the quality of urban life as well as a willingness to act on visions of a better Chicago characterize the 1890s as a turning point in the city's history. As the problems of the 1890s emerged so did the impetus for action to solve them.

A City of a Million Strangers

The dynamism of Chicago's economy lured thousands of newcomers from all over the country and the world each year. Be it the dream of making millions or of acquiring a modest home, the city held the prospect of a better life. Most adult Chicagoans had not been born in the city, and over a third of Chicago's more than one million inhabitants were foreign-born. In the 1890s Germans formed the largest group of immigrants in Chicago, and many Irish, Scandinavians, and Poles lived there as well. Chicagoans, however, had come from virtually every European country. A survey conducted in 1903 by University of Chicago professor Carl Buck revealed that forty languages were spoken in the city, fourteen of them by more than ten thousand people each.[3]

The sizes of different immigrant groups reflected, in part, the different periods when people came to Chicago. Irish and Germans first came to Chicago in large groups in the 1850s, Scandinavians began to come in large numbers in the 1860s, Bohemians in the 1870s, Poles in the

1880s, and eastern European Jews and Italians in the 1890s. Although people from northern and western Europe continued to immigrate to Chicago in the 1890s, larger numbers were coming from eastern and southern Europe. The timing of these waves of immigration depended on conditions in specific countries. The Irish and the Swedes (the most numerous of the Scandinavians) had been pushed out of their homelands in the middle of the nineteenth century by famine, as the rural economies of both countries collapsed. In the 1890s the decline of peasant agriculture, growing populations, and the slow pace of industrial development in southern Italy and many parts of eastern Europe increased the number of emigrants from these countries.[4]

Because most immigrants were poor, they settled first in the tenement districts that ringed the downtown business district. If they prospered they usually moved to better housing in other areas. In the 1890s the newest immigrants to Chicago from southern and eastern Europe crowded together west of the downtown in the area bounded by Polk, Twelfth, Halsted, and Canal streets, known as Chicago's "port of entry." The cheap housing of the tenements there was close to the train stations where immigrants arrived in the city and close to the labor exchanges that directed them to jobs. These immigrants started where the Irish and

---

20   A SKETCH OF THE LINGUISTIC CONDITIONS OF CHICAGO

In the following table the languages are given in the order of their numerical strength in Chicago, so far as this can be determined. As explained before, the numbers are only approximate. The asterisks indicate those languages, already named, which are spoken by greater numbers in Chicago than in other cities of this country:

	about		about
German	500,000	Chinese	} 1,000
* Polish	125,000	Spanish	
* Swedish	100,000	Finnish	} 500
* Bohemian	90,000	Scotch Gaelic	
* Norwegian	50,000	Lettic	
Yiddish	50,000	Arabic	250
* Dutch	35,000	Armenian	} 100
Italian	25,000	Manx	
* Danish	20,000	Icelandic	
French	15,000	Albanian	
Irish	10,000	Bulgarian	
* Croatian and Servian	10,000	Turkish	
* Slovakian	10,000	Japanese	less than 100
* Lithuanian	10,000	Portuguese	
Russian	7,000	Breton	
Hungarian	5,000	Esthonian	
* Greek	4,000	Basque	
Frisian	} 1,000 to 2,000	Gypsy	
Roumanian			
Welsh			
Slovenian			
Flemish			

Immigration had made Chicago a tower of Babel, as University of Chicago professor Carl Buck discovered in his 1903 investigation.

*The downtown skyscrapers were the head-
quarters of the economic activities that
attracted thousands of newcomers to the
city each year. LaSalle Street Tunnel from
Randolph.*

*Immigrants brought objects to preserve their
religious and ethnic traditions. Left to right.
Christian items: statue of Christ (Polish);
Communion chalice; Bible (German, 1866);
rosary (Lithuanian). Jewish items: menorah
(Polish); prayer shawl; Kiddush cup (German). Swedish items: wooden bowl (1859);
woman's clogs; flax chopper (1865); painted
child's chair.*

Swedes had decades before—at the bottom. Because food was cheap, the new immigrants could survive, but they crowded into the worst slums and had the worst jobs. For poorer immigrants, proximity to work was a key factor in choosing housing. By the 1890s the major Polish settlement in Chicago centered at Division Street and Ashland Avenue, but four other concentrations of Poles had grown near the sites of major industries, such as the steel mills in South Chicago.[5]

As immigrants prospered they looked for better housing away from the slums and the factories. German immigrants and their children settled large areas of the city's North Side, especially Lakeview and Ravenswood. By 1900 the largest predominantly German area, between Chicago and Fullerton avenues from the lake to the river, was practically self-sufficient in retail businesses, services, hospitals, schools, churches, orphanages, clubs, lodging houses, and amusements.[6] Residential exclusiveness by nationality was not the norm, however. The Irish lived in virtually all areas of the city, while many of the Swedes and Norwegians settled among the Germans on the North Side. Increasingly builders were creating class-segregated neighborhoods by clustering housing in narrow price ranges. As immigrants chose housing according to their means, they often found themselves among people of different cultures but similar pocketbooks.

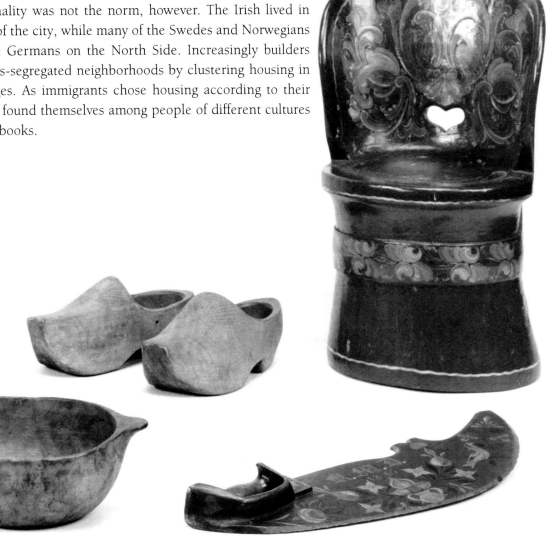

Panorama of Chicago. From Monadnock Block, Dearborn, Jackson, Van Buren streets and Custom House Place. Color lithograph by George W. Melville, 1897. [Plate 3]

Chicago Neighborhoods in the 1890s

1. Black ghetto
2. German Neighborhood
3. Lakeview
4. Maxwell St./"port of entry"
5. Polish "downtown"
6. Pullman
7. Ravenswood
8. South Chicago
9. Union Stockyards

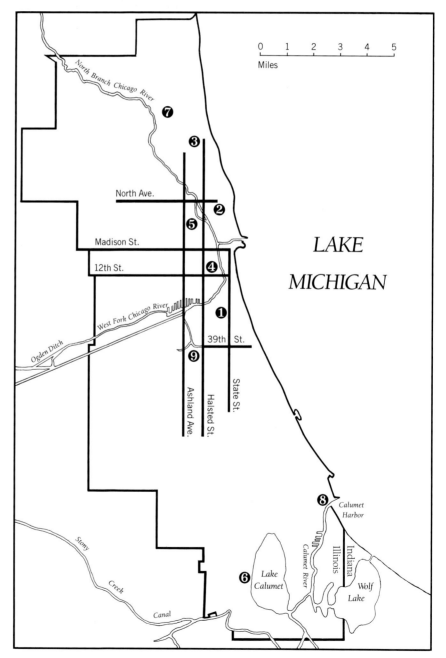

The diversity of the population created a cosmopolitan environment, different from that of the small towns and rural areas of America and Europe from which the immigrants had come. Chicago was not, however, a melting pot. The city was more like a container in which divergent groups developed their own cultures, organizations, and customs. Americans from the Northeast who settled Chicago before the Civil War set the model: limit government activity and develop private community institutions to meet citizens' needs. Private individuals who would benefit by them were expected to pay for all or part of city improvements or services. Any activity that could be left to individuals, families, churches, or private businesses should be.[7] Later arrivals followed this pattern and established their own organizations for social, religious, and philanthropic purposes. Immigrants embraced American political ideals, construing democracy and individual rights as guarantees of both the right to political participation and the right to maintain their cultural distinctiveness. In the 1890s three-quarters of Chicagoans were immigrants or the children of immigrants, and their desire for cultural continuity made the city a mosaic of diverse ethnic communities.

Creating Communities   Immigrant groups preserved their cultural communities primarily through families and institutions rather than through residential segregation. They usually created religious institutions first; in an alien environment this source of support and guidance became even more important than in the homeland. The northeasterners who had settled Chicago in the first half of the nineteenth century were predominantly Protestant, and they formed Presbyterian, Methodist, Baptist, Episcopalian, and other congregations. The influx of German and Scandinavian Lutherans brought a new diversity to the religious life of the city, as they founded congregations with services in their own languages.[8]

Although immigration brought many Protestants to Chicago, it brought even more Catholics and Jews. When the Irish and German Catholics arrived in the city in the 1850s, they had to build religious institutions from scratch. Irish and Irish-American archbishops led the diocese of Chicago for most of the nineteenth century. By the 1890s Roman Catholics outnumbered Protestants or Jews in Chicago. Immigration, however, brought new ethnic diversity to Chicago Catholics.[9]

Most of the newest immigrants to Chicago in the 1890s were Roman Catholics, but they were from southern and eastern Europe, and they found the existing churches inhospitable to their languages or cultures

*Anna May Aubry celebrated her first com-
munion at St. Jean Baptiste, a French-
Canadian Catholic parish, when it opened in
1892. Below: Archbishop Patrick A. Feehan
headed the Roman Catholic Archdiocese of
Chicago between 1880 and 1902.*

*Facing page, top: German Jews first settled
in Chicago in the 1850s. Their oldest congregation, Kehilath Anshe Mayriv, commissioned this new temple (1892), designed by
Dankmar Adler. Eastern European Jews,
more orthodox and much poorer than the
German Jews, lived and worked near Maxwell Street (facing page). Front of Jewish to-
bacconists' store, Maxwell Street, c. 1906.*

because so many parishes were Irish. Archbishop Patrick Feehan maintained unity in much the same way the rest of the city did, by encouraging separation and local control under a loose unifying structure. Within
the boundaries of an existing parish, the archdiocese allowed the construction of several ethnic churches. In the 1890s forty-one Roman
Catholic churches were built in Chicago, all but seven of them identifia-
bly ethnic parishes.[10] An ethnic church was usually named for the saint
most important to the national group it served, like the French Canadian
church, St. Jean Baptiste, which opened in 1892. Religious practices
particular to each culture were tolerated, and the Italians re-created
their distinctive street parades for the feasts of saints.

The first large group of Jews who came to Chicago were German, and
by the 1890s many of them had prospered. The first Jewish congregation
in Chicago, Kehilath Anshe Mayriv (K.A.M.), celebrated its fiftieth anniversary in 1897. It commissioned a new building to be designed by
Dankmar Adler, one of Chicago's leading architects and son of a K.A.M.
rabbi.[11] In the 1890s large numbers of Jews from eastern Europe poured
into the city. Unlike the German Jews, the new immigrants were poor,
spoke Yiddish, and followed more orthodox religious practices. The
eastern European Jews clustered around Maxwell Street—the slum street
where the poor bought and sold the city's second-hand goods and left-
overs. Their storefront synagogues, marriage arrangement bureaus, He-
brew schools, matzo bakeries, and kosher butcher shops revealed yet
another community forming within the city. In the 1890s religious, linguistic, and class differences kept German Jews and eastern European
Jews at odds. In 1900, however, they united to form a common philanthropic agency, the Associated Jewish Charities.[12]

German culture and nationalism were not tied to any one religion,
and German Protestants, Catholics, and Jews who practiced their religions separately were all active in the German cultural community.
For other immigrants, such as Poles and the Irish, religion connected
directly to ethnic identity. As an integral component of the fight against
Protestant England, Catholicism became an essential aspect of Irish national identity, and it remained part of Irish-American identity. In the
Polish community Father Vincent Barzynski attempted to make St. Stanislaus Kostka, the first and largest of the Polish parishes, a total community that would meet all the needs of its members. By the 1890s the
church had built a complex with a parish hall for group meetings, a
gymnasium, a parish school, and two facilities for advanced education:
Holy Family Academy and the College of St. Stanislaus.

While religion could unite individuals of the same ethnic group, it could also divide them. Polish anticlerical nationalists and church leaders vied for the leadership of Poles in America, and they founded competing fraternal orders, the secular Polish National Alliance and the Polish Roman Catholic Union. These mutual benefit societies grew rapidly but remained hostile to each other for many years. Differences between Polish Catholics also led to a schism and the formation of the Independent Polish Catholic Church and the Polish National Catholic Church. In the 1890s the Polish community in Chicago was focused inward on these issues that emanated from the homeland.[13]

Like native-born Americans who migrated to big cities, the immigrants found, however, that to re-create the intimacy and supportiveness

Newspapers, mixing news of the community with news of the homeland and the world, were the vital communication link within the ethnic communities. These newspapers in German, Yiddish, Italian, Swedish, Norwegian, and English are but a few of the many published in Chicago in the 1890s.

of the small town or village, they needed new institutions that few had known previously. Newspapers replaced the gossip network of the small town, and the ethnic press mixed news of the ethnic community with news of the homeland and the world. The largest immigrant group, the Germans, supported twenty newspapers published in Chicago in the 1890s. Fraternal organizations and other social clubs cemented the bonds within immigrant groups.

Mutual benefit societies and homes for the elderly supplied the care in times of adversity that extended families or communities might have provided in the homeland. The German Mutual Benefit and Aid Society, for instance, provided medical benefits or funeral expenses for members in return for their dues, and the Altenheim cared for the elderly. Virtually all social services in Chicago were provided privately; as each immigrant group grew and prospered, it created a more extensive network of services and institutions, including hospitals and orphanages. Initially social services were supported by individual contributions and membership dues. As the network of services proliferated, so did fund-raising events like the annual German-American Charity Ball or the Swedes' Augustana Hospital Bazaar.

The cultural forms that were taken for granted in the homeland had to be institutionalized if they were to persist in the cultural maelstrom of Chicago. To hear familiar music, read familiar books, and see familiar plays performed in their own languages, the immigrants formed numer-

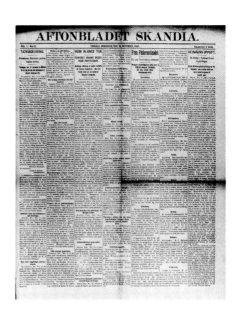

Left: Residents of Altenheim, c. 1890. In the cities of America new institutions, like homes for the elderly, provided the support that kin networks or neighbors had provided in the rural areas and small towns from which the immigrants often came.

ous singing societies, libraries, and theater groups. As befitted their numbers, the Germans had the largest number of such institutions. The demand for plays performed in German was large enough to support a theater building, Germania Hall. The German community supported concerts by professional German musicians and singers as well as non-professional local groups like the Germania Maennerchor, the city's

German Chicagoans supported twenty newspapers in the 1890s, but the Illinois Staats
Zeitung (above), which celebrated its fiftieth
anniversary in 1898, had the largest circula-
tion. [Plate 2]

German Chicagoans supported educational
programs in their own language at all levels.
In 1897 they formed a German-American
University.

most famous German choir. Florence Ziegfeld, Sr., a well-known music
teacher and founder of the Chicago Musical College, promoted many
concerts featuring German music and German artists.

German immigrants also contributed two new cultural forms to Chicago: the turnverein and the beer garden. The aim of the Turner movement, which began in Berlin in 1811, was to create well-rounded
individuals, healthy in mind and body, who would be informed, active
citizens.[14] The vehicle for this was the turnverein, a social and athletic
club that combined lectures and discussions with physical activity,
stressing gymnastics and military drill. German monarchs who feared
its democratic potential had suppressed the movement until 1842. It
flourished among German-Americans, who saw its goals as particularly
suited to their new situation. American cities offered political rights and
responsibilities but few outlets for physical recreation. The many turnverein formed by German Chicagoans since the 1850s were a leading
force in encouraging sports and physical recreation in the city.

The second German institution, the beer garden, became a favorite
recreation spot for many Chicagoans. Beer gardens differed from Chicago's all-male saloons. Women and children were welcome, appropriate music and entertainment were provided, and unlike saloons there
was no hint of the disreputable.[15] Initially the German practice of going
to the beer garden on Sunday afternoon aroused much opposition from
American Protestants who objected to nonreligious activities on the
Christian Sabbath. But by the 1890s, beer gardens could be found
throughout the predominantly German North Side, as well as along the
lake and, for those who wanted a day in the country, in the suburbs at
the end of the streetcar lines.

A key to maintaining culture was language, and immigrants supported
many private schools that taught in their native languages. Because of its
size and political strength, the German community persuaded the Chicago Board of Education to provide German language instruction in the
public schools for those who desired it. In 1892–93, 44,270 children
studied German in the third through eighth grades.[16] While most groups
supported foreign-language schools only at the primary level, German
Chicagoans attempted to form a German-American University in the
1890s, but it did not succeed. Very few Chicagoans of any group went to
college in the 1890s, and apparently the German-American University
could not attract enough students.

Immigrants had a profound effect on Chicago's politics. Both Democrats and Republicans encouraged immigrants to organize party affiliates

Left: A German form of recreation, the beer garden became popular in America. While American saloons were for men, the beer garden was suitable for the family. Bismark Garden, Chicago, 1906.

Below: The German turnverein was a social club that encouraged physical recreation, especially gymnastics. German immigrants to Chicago formed many of these societies in an effort to maintain their German culture. Members of the Chicago Turn Gemeinde are shown here in 1893 celebrating the group's fortieth anniversary.

Although the Irish dominated the Democratic party of Chicago for decades, the first Irish Catholic mayor was John P. Hopkins (above) from 1893 to 1895.

within their own groups, and each party made sure to balance their ticket with representatives of any ethnic group that had sizable voting strength. Fluency in the English language and knowledge of English government forms prepared the Irish to take full advantage of the political opportunities in America. In the 1850s the Irish gravitated to the Democratic party, and by the 1890s they controlled it in Chicago. A disproportionate number of Chicago's elected officials were Irish-American, and jobs on the police force and in municipal departments were important stepping stones away from the poverty of their early years in the city. John Hopkins, the first Irish Catholic mayor of Chicago, held office from 1893 to 1895. The best-known Irish politicians, however, were the notoriously corrupt aldermen—"Bathhouse" John Coughlin, Michael "Hinky Dink" Kenna, and John Powers.[17]

While immigrants shaped mainstream politics, they also made Chicago a center of radical politics. Reflecting the extensive industrial development in Germany and the strength of the socialist movement there, German workers in Chicago took an early and active role in creating the city's many trade unions and radical political groups; they formed the majority of the Socialist Labor party and the Chicago anarchist move-

German workers in Chicago brought not only their craft skills from their homeland, but also their politics. Until the mid-1890s the primary support for socialism in Chicago was among German-speaking immigrants. German Socialist flag, 1892.

ment of the 1880s, although Bohemians, Scandinavians, and others also joined.[18]

While each group perpetuated a different culture, the patterns of community development were strikingly similar. Those groups that had been in the city longest had the broadest range of community institutions, but newer groups replicated the same pattern over time. By the 1890s Germans had created virtually a city within a city. Germans of all religions, classes, and political persuasions created a German version of every type of organization in the city. New groups, like Italians, had only begun the process, concentrating on religious facilities, immigrant aid societies, newspapers, and mutual aid societies. This relatively uniform pattern of community development reflected the impact of the new urban environment on the immigrants. In the big city people created institutions to meet needs that previously were handled by more informal methods, such as kinship or neighborly sharing, in small communities. Although mutual aid societies had just begun in southern Italy in the 1890s, for instance, the Italians in Chicago formed many of them. The Italian press of Chicago also was without precedent for most of these immigrants, who had had no newspapers or been illiterate at home.[19]

The urge to retain their specific national identities ran strong among immigrants, and nationalism was an important component of ethnic culture. The fight for independence from England was an active concern of Chicago's Irish community, supported by members of the Clan na Gael, the Irish Nationalists of Chicago, and the Central Parnell League.[20] In the early years when their numbers were small, Swedes, Norwegians, and Danes often joined the same groups or participated in the same activities. Scandinavianism, which grew in importance in their homelands, found little support in Chicago, however. As their numbers increased, Swedes, Danes, and Norwegians clung to their separate national identities.[21]

Despite the desire for cultural continuity, the nature of developing a new community meant that the culture of the immigrants was not preserved but transformed to combine elements of the homeland and the distinct impress of America. The organizations of Scandinavians reflected the variety of experiences of Chicago's immigrants: not only contact with several cultures, but also for most the movement from the small town to the big city. Most Swedish immigrants came from rural areas and had never belonged to social, fraternal, or cultural organizations. Such organizations in Sweden were formed by the urban middle class. In Chicago, however, Swedes joined many groups. Chicago's Scandina-

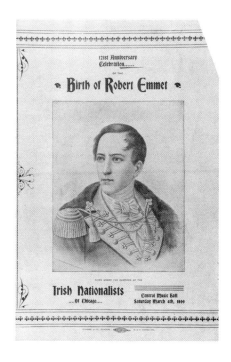

Irish nationalism was central to ethnic identity among Irish-Americans in Chicago. They actively supported the fight for independence from England, establishing in Chicago the Irish Nationalists (above) and the Central Parnell League (below).

Den Norske Turnforening of Chicago
—HOLD THEIR GRAND—
TURNERS' FESTIVAL!
(Turnfest) and
★ **PIC-NIC** ★
At the Beautiful PALOS PARK
ON THE WABASH RAILWAY.
Sunday. July 27th, 1890.

PROGRAMME.
Turning on Horizontal and Parallel Bars.—Somersaults.—Pyramids.
—Vaulting.—Brother Acts.—Singing.—Dancing.
RACES:
1. Boys under 10 years. Prize, Base Ball and Bat.
2. Girls under 10 years. Prize, Doll.
3. Ladies' Race. 1st Prize, Fancy Fan. 2nd Prize, Fine Autograph
   Album.
4. Gentlemen's Race. 1st Prize, Fancy Smoking Pipe. 2nd Prize,
   Fancy Match safe.
5. Turners' Sack Run. 1st Prize, Turners' Fancy Silk Belt. 2nd
   Prize, a box of Cigars.

Train leaves the Grand Trunk Depot at 9 A. M. sharp, and Palos
Park at 7 P. M. sharp.

Tickets only 50 cents
for Round Trip Fare and Admission to Park.

For Sale by: Baltzer Haugen & Co., 484 Milwaukee Avenue.— O. C. Land
229 Milwaukee Ave.— Isac Rasmussen, 274 W. Indiana Street, and
M. Kean, 102 W. Huron St.,

Come out with the Popular Turners and have a good time!

Above: The Danes and others adopted the German turnverein, as through contact with others and the demands of urban life, the cultures of immigrant groups changed.

vians followed their own traditions when they founded sharpshooter societies, but a German model when they created turnverein. The Scandinavians followed an American model for fraternal organizations when they founded ethnic lodges of the Odd Fellows. The story, however, was often more complex. The American temperance organization, the International Order of Good Templars, was organized in Norway in 1878. Norwegian immigrants who had been Good Templars at home later started Norden, the Norwegian Good Templar Lodge in Chicago.[22]

What Was An American?   Chicago's ethnic groups often disliked each other, and rivalries always existed. Those who identified themselves as Americans were often hostile to immigrants. Derogatory ethnic stereotyping abounded, and the use of epithets like ''dago'' for Italian was commonplace.[23] The Irish were often depicted as barely human in popular cartoons. During the depression of the mid-1890s, these hostil-

A GOOD DISGUISE.

MR. BRADY (in the French Exhibit, reading).— ''Mask of Michael Angelo.'' Will, Moike, me bye,
yez knew your business. No man would iver recognoize an Oirishman under sich a fahlse-face as thot.

Right: Ethnic stereotypes and insults were prevalent in Chicago in the 1890s and were often the subject of humor magazines. World's Fair Puck, Sept. 25, 1893.

The Americans from New England and the Middle Atlantic states who settled Chicago in the early nineteenth century brought with them the social organizations, like the Masons, that were so popular in the East.

ities reached a new level. A nativist reaction to immigrants in general and to the new immigrants from southern and eastern Europe in particular formed across the country.[24] Calls for immigration restriction gained support, as many native-born Americans championed a new kind of nationalism that identified the newcomers as threats to American society. In Chicago appeals to Americanism shaped politics, and suspicion and discrimination hampered the possibility for civic unity. For most of the nineteenth century, the definition of Americanism focused on the political ideology of republicanism: Americans were free people who had political rights that had been denied to the masses of Europeans. In the 1890s, however, this concept of Americanism was superceded by a cultural bias later characterized as white Anglo-Saxon Protestantism.

Like the immigrants, most adult Chicagoans who were native-born Americans with native-born parents had migrated to the city, primarily from New England and the Middle Atlantic states. In the 1890s they composed less than a quarter of Chicago's population, but they created numerous Protestant churches and a full range of fraternal and benevolent societies, such as the Masons. Although immigrants were not welcome, these organizations were open to their children who desired to join groups outside their ethnic communities. The native-born felt increasingly outnumbered however, and reacted by claiming the mantle of Americanism. They rejected the immigrants' right to maintain their

The nativist reaction of the 1890s swelled in Chicago during George Swift's 1895 mayoral campaign.

HEADQUARTERS

LOYAL AMERICAN LEGION

MASONIC TEMPLE.

Personal and
Confidential ..

Attention Voters of American Birth and Ideas.

DEAR SIR:

        Your name has been sent to us by a friend of our order as a proper person to send this letter to. As you know, we have an important election next Tuesday, April 2, an election which all good Americans ought to take an interest in. Why? For the past eighteen months this city has had an Irish Mayor, and now they want to give us a German Mayor in the person of Frank Wenter, the Democratic candidate for that office.

        For a great many years this city has been governed by foreign- erns, and **IT IS NOW TIME TO CALL A HALT.** The Irish are good enough in their place, and so are the Germans, but neither of these nationalities ought to be allowed to name a Mayor for a great city like Chicago. **Please keep this matter to yourself and uphold our American Institutions,** and let the foreigners take care of their own business, and allow the government of this city to be run by people who were born here. In other words, vote for

GEORGE B. SWIFT,

the candidate of all **TRUE AMERICANS** for Mayor.

-Polls open at 6 a. m. and close at 4 p. m., Tuesday, April 2. Vote early on that date and bring your friends to vote for George B. Swift.

EXECUTIVE COMMITTEE.

cultural identities, and they began to demand cultural assimilation. They founded new groups, such as the Sons of the American Revolution, that defined *American* in terms of lineage. These groups equated patriotism with genealogy and cultivated a restricted sense of nationality that excluded not only the immigrants but also their children.

George Swift ran his 1895 campaign for mayor on the platform of nativism and appealed frankly for the votes of the native-born. Swift's supporters argued:

The Irish are good enough in their place, and so are the Germans; but neither of these nationalities ought to be allowed to name a Mayor for a great city like Chicago. . . . Let the foreigners take care of their own business, and allow the government of this city to be run by people who were born here.[25]

An important part of the cultural conflict of the 1890s between the native-born and the immigrants was anti-Catholicism. As more and more Catholic immigrants entered the country, Americanism became more closely linked with Protestantism. Tensions between Protestants and Catholics grew in Chicago in the 1880s and 1890s as successful Irish-Americans moved into previously Protestant neighborhoods and built new churches and parochial schools.[26] The American Protective Association (APA), which led the anti-Catholic crusade nationwide, was not strong in Chicago, but local Democrats worried about its potential growth. Chicago businessman Paul Morton cautioned his father, Secretary of Agriculture J. Sterling Morton, about the composition of political appointments in 1893, emphasizing the strength of the APA in southern Illinois. Hoping the national level of the Democratic party would exercise caution, Paul Morton wrote:

The point I want to make in writing you is that too many Irishmen and especially too many Catholics will be a grave mistake in the Chicago appointments. . . . The Republicans very frequently put a Catholic Irishman or a Catholic German on their tickets, but they always avoid having the ticket dominated by them.[27]

Americans, White and Black   The native-born Americans of native-born parents, however, were not a united group in Chicago. As in the rest of America, they were divided by race. Since Reconstruction, African-Americans had had voting rights in Illinois, and they had won state civil rights legislation outlawing segregation and discrimination in

In the 1890s native-born Americans of native-born parents began to define American in terms of lineage, and they flocked to new organizations, like the Sons of the American Revolution.

In 1893 Ida B. Wells (above) came to Chicago where she continued her crusade against lynching and fought the increasing racism directed against African-Americans in the city.

Above: Black doll. African-Americans came to Chicago from the South in increasing numbers in the 1890s to build families where they thought they would have greater opportunity. [Plate 4]

public accommodations. Private groups, such as churches and fraternal and benevolent associations, were usually segregated, however. Most whites rejected the concept of integration, which African-Americans espoused. Though they composed less than 2 percent of all Chicagoans, African-Americans had no choice but to form their own private organizations. The black community supported over a dozen churches by 1900, all but one of them Protestant. Social groups, singing societies, and fraternal orders were numerous, and the *Lakeside City Directory* printed a separate list of over sixty "colored societies," most of them groups, like the Masons and Odd Fellows, that flourished among white Chicagoans too.[28]

Racism became more intense throughout the United States in the 1890s. A new generation of African-Americans, born in freedom, came of age in the South at the time that white southerners established Jim Crow laws to segregate and disenfranchise them. These young people left the South for cities like Chicago to find the opportunities they were denied at home. The black population of Chicago more than doubled in the 1890s because of migration, especially from the upper South and border states.[29] Many of the future leaders of the black community of Chicago were among these migrants. Thirty-year-old Ida B. Wells was forced to leave Memphis, Tennessee, fearing for her safety, because of her nationally known crusade to stop lynching. She moved to Chicago in 1893, and, while she continued to fight lynching, she also became vitally involved in local issues. Other newcomers in the 1890s included Robert Abbott, who founded the *Chicago Defender*; Jesse Binga, who founded the first black-owned bank in the city; and the Reverend Archibald Carey, who led many civic and political movements in the early twentieth century.

These young African-Americans did not, however, find a refuge in the North. As the black population in Chicago grew, it met with greater hostility from the white population. Among most whites racism elicited no shame. Major newspapers published racist stories and jokes, such as those of George Ade, one of Chicago's most celebrated journalists. One of Ida B. Wells's first activities in Chicago was to protest discrimination at the World's Columbian Exposition. In the book, *The Reason Why the Colored American is not in the World's Columbian Exposition*, she and her future husband, Ferdinand Barnett, showed that the fair excluded the achievements of African-Americans, hired few of them and only for the most menial jobs, and allowed black visitors to eat only at the Haitian exhibit.[30]

In the 1890s African-Americans in Chicago found themselves the objects of discrimination in public accommodations, despite civil rights legislation. The law's small fines for noncompliance did not deter many restaurants and hotels from refusing to serve African-Americans.[31] Discrimination in housing also increased. By 1900 an area of black settlement had developed from Twelfth to Thirty-ninth streets east of Wentworth Avenue and west of Wabash Avenue. This neighborhood formed the nucleus of Chicago's twentieth-century black ghetto. Discrimination in employment had always existed, and African-Americans were unable to get industrial jobs, the growth sector of Chicago's economy. Instead most found jobs only as domestic servants or day laborers.

In the 1890s African-Americans persisted in the demand for equal rights, and Wells helped organize equal rights organizations, like the Afro-American Council in 1898. More and more, however, black Chicagoans came to doubt whether equal access to white-dominated institutions would be granted. Before the 1890s every attempt to form separate black institutions was regarded by community leaders as self-segregation and contrary to the goal of integration. In the 1890s, however, Chicago's African-Americans began to build their own institutions, which would serve them for the next century. The most important of these was Provident Hospital. Most Chicago hospitals would neither allow black doctors and nurses to practice nor black patients to have private rooms. Community leaders organized by Dr. Daniel Hale Williams, the best-known black physician in the country and an outstanding surgeon, cre-

"TOO SICK TO WUHK"

Racism found expression everywhere, as in this illustration (above) from George Ade's Pink Marsh, *1897.*

Below: Provident Hospital nurses, c. 1900. Provident Hospital was the only facility at which black women could train as nurses.

Dr. Daniel Hale Williams (above) founded Provident Hospital in 1891 because other Chicago hospitals would not allow black doctors or nurses to practice or black patients to have private rooms.

Residential segregation increased in the 1890s, and the South Side black ghetto, bounded by Twelfth and Thirty-ninth streets and Wentworth and Wabash avenues, developed. Olivet Baptist Church, Dearborn and Twenty-seventh streets, 1905.

ated Provident Hospital in 1891. Although organized as a reaction to racism, the hospital was more than the mirror image of white hospitals. In its policy of openness to staff of all races, it reflected the desire for equal access and a vision of an integrated society. The hospital began in a small apartment building but moved to a new building with a separate nursing school in 1896. Financial support for Provident came not only from the black community but also from major Chicago business leaders such as George Pullman, Philip Armour, and Marshall Field. Provident became the major health facility for African-Americans in Chicago, and its school the only place black women could train as nurses.

The paucity of other social services to serve African-Americans spurred action in the 1890s. Ida B. Wells formed the first Negro Woman's Club in Chicago, organized a kindergarten for black children, and established an employment service for new migrants.[32] The Reverend Reverdy Ransom, another young newcomer, began the first social settlement for African-Americans, the Institutional Church and Social Settlement. While providing activities for all age groups, the Institutional Church responded strongly to the needs of children and youth in the city. It had a day nursery, a gymnasium, club activities for children and adults, and music classes.

The process of building separate community organizations among African-Americans culminated in the 1920s when a city within a city, the "Black Belt" of Chicago's South Side, formed. While the children of the white immigrants increasingly joined nonethnic organizations and moved away from ethnic neighborhoods, the depth of white racism denied this opportunity to the children of black Chicagoans. The allegiance to ethnic cultures was strongest among the white immigrants themselves, but the rejection of white culture and the affirmation of black culture grew with the new generation born and raised in the ghetto.

The City, Not the Neighborhood   Ethnic and racial communities were an important component of Chicago in the 1890s. Not everyone chose to live within these confines, however, and even people who valued the ethnic community often found it necessary to join others outside their group. The political parties and the Roman Catholic Church already provided models of how to achieve unity through the recognition of separate groups. In the 1890s Chicagoans found such models increasingly relevant, as they confronted the physical problems of unrestrained urban growth and industrial development. The streets

were dirty, dangerous, and inconvenient; a pall of smoke hung over large areas of the city; and the stench of garbage, chemicals, and other industrial pollution was virtually everywhere. A visiting Englishman described Chicago as "queen and guttersnipe of cities, cynosure and cesspool of the world!"[33] While the standard of living for Chicagoans varied from wealth to poverty, none enjoyed a clean, safe environment.

Chicago lacked an adequate sewer system, and by the late 1880s the results were disease and death for city residents. In 1891 typhoid alone killed almost two thousand Chicagoans.[34] Cholera and other water-borne diseases were rampant. The wretched condition of the streets exacerbated the public health problem. The private firms that obtained

Congestion plagued the downtown streets in the 1890s as streetcars, carriages, wagons, and pedestrians all converged on the densely developed city center. Traffic jam on Dearborn Street looking south from Randolph Street, 1909.

SUGGESTIONS
... FOR ...
Preventing Cholera.

1ST. PURE AIR.
     Keep windows open. Air beds thoroughly every day. Exercise freely out of doors.

2ND. PURE WATER.
     Boil the lake water for one half hour, then put to cool in, a stone jar, placing over the top a flannel cloth. Ice water is dangerous.

TEMPERANCE.
     Be moderate in eating and drinking. Beware of over-ripe fruits and vegetables. Cook vegetables and fruits until thoroughly done. Beer and whiskey drinkers become the plague's first victims. It is safer to let alcoholic drinks alone.

CLEANLINESS.
     Dirt is one of the causes of Cholera, therefore keep the person, the house, and the yard well rid of it. Clean out the dark and damp hidden places, burn garbage, clean cess-pools, or report to City Health department. White wash walls, fences and out houses.

RECIPE FOR WHITEWASH.
     Mix lime and water until thick enough to use as paint, in this dissolve one pound of salt and use freely, for both lime and salt are cleansing.

A·REMEDY.
     Three teaspoonfuls of diluted Sulphuric Acid in a quart of boiled water—sweetened to taste, makes a good drink and cures Cholera.

Sept. 1892

Above: Because Chicago lacked an adequate sewer system, epidemic diseases like typhoid and cholera plagued the city in the 1890s. Hull-House broadside, 1892.

the contracts for garbage collection and street cleaning through kickbacks and graft saw no need to provide good service. In the tenement areas, "the streets were paved with wooden blocks, and after a heavy rainfall the blocks would become loose and float about in the street. During the drying process the stench was nauseating. There were many places where the blocks did not return to their mooring and smelly water would remain for days."[35] While disease was worst in the tenement districts, the contagion spread to all neighborhoods. The public health problem could only be solved by the city: a mutual benefit society could help pay medical expenses, but it could not prevent disease.

Chicago's streets were also dangerous. Streetcar and railroad tracks were laid in the streets, and neither underpasses nor overpasses existed to assist pedestrians attempting to cross the tracks. Many pedestrians were struck, and accidents occurred when streetcars jumped the tracks. Chicago had a "multitude of mutilated people," whose misfortune supported a large industry in artificial limbs and crutches.[36] Nor did the streetcars provide good service. High fares and crowding were the rule. To save on conductors' salaries, companies refused to use extra cars at peak periods. These conditions persisted because the streetcar companies bribed city officials to get their way. Not only the poor,

Right: Garbage filled city streets and alleys because the private companies that contracted with the city to clean the streets found that bribing aldermen was cheaper than actually doing the job. Alley south of Van Buren Street looking east from Halsted Street, 1910.

but also the prosperous who had moved away from the factories and the downtown where they worked, relied on the streetcars.

Pure water, sanitation, paved streets, and safe, efficient transportation barely existed because of the tradition of limited government. Chicago's government resembled that of other American cities in its limited scope. Services and utilities were provided, wherever possible, by letting contracts to private firms rather than by the government itself. In large cities like Chicago where extensive utilities and services were a necessity, limited government had a price—corruption. Chicago's aldermen awarded contracts to those who bribed them the most, and the public was cynical about any government undertaking.[37] While Chicagoans clamored for better city services and public utilities in the 1890s, they could not find a way to provide them without first attacking the graft endemic to their political system.

Just as individual groups could not solve the physical problems of the city, they were relatively powerless against other city blights. Many Chicagoans deplored the moral health of the city and sought to protect their children from vice. Even if they could keep vice out of their own neighborhoods, parents could not protect older children from the knowledge that drunkenness, gambling, and prostitution were rampant

Above: The streetcars often struck pedestrians or jumped the tracks, injuring employees and riders. The Graphic, *March 18, 1893. Below left: This 1885 catalog demonstrates the thriving business in artificial limbs, attesting to the danger of the streetcars and railroads that crisscrossed the city.*

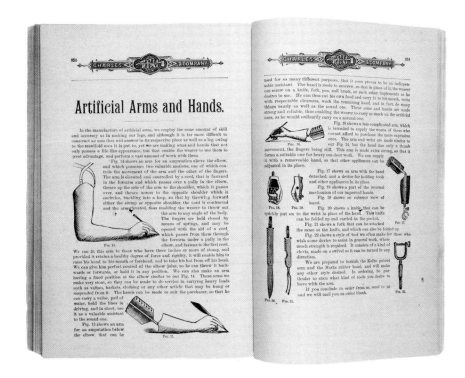

*Above, right and facing page, top: Vice oper-
ated openly in Chicago. The most expensive
brothel, the Everleigh Club, distributed a
promotional brochure when it redecorated in
1902. English reformer William Stead
mapped the Levee, Chicago's world-famous
vice district, for his 1894 exposé,* If Christ
Came to Chicago. *Above: "Bathhouse" John
Coughlin, a First Ward alderman, protected
the Levee and made a fortune from the
bribes made by private companies to Chicago's aldermen. Below: Michael "Hinky
Dink" Kenna, also a First Ward alderman,
owned a saloon that served the largest
schooners of beer in town.*

The Everleigh Club

WHILE not an extremely imposing edifice without, is a most sumptuous
place within. 2131 Dearborn Street, Chicago, has long been famed
for its luxurious furnishings, famous paintings and statuary, and its elaborate and
artistic decorations. "The New Annex" 2133 Dearborn Street, formally
opened November 1, 1902, has added prestige to the club, and won admira-
tion and praise from all visitors. With double front entrances, the twin
buildings within are so connected as to seem as one. Steam heat throughout,
with electric fans in summer; one never feels the winter's chill or summer's
heat in this luxurious resort. Fortunate indeed, with all the comforts of life
surrounding them, are the members of the Everleigh Club.

This little booklet will convey but a faint idea of the magnificence of the
club and its appointments.

in other parts of the city. Chicago's red light district, the Levee, was
famous throughout the United States and had become a major tourist
attraction. The most notorious of the brothels was operated by the Everleigh sisters; patrons expected to spend several hundred dollars on
one night's amusement. The Levee, located in the First Ward between
Eighteenth and Twenty-fourth streets from Dearborn Street to the Illinois Central railroad tracks, had something for every taste and pock-
etbook. The brothels, saloons, and gambling dens of the Levee received
protection from their aldermen, Michael "Hinky Dink" Kenna and
"Bathhouse" John Coughlin, for a price.[38]

Although moral corruption was concentrated in the vice district,
drinking, gambling, and prostitution existed throughout the city. Much
concern focused on the ubiquitous saloon. The city's fanciest saloons,
such as Hannah and Hogg on West Madison Street in the Loop, were
elegantly furnished with stained glass and marble; lavishly decorated
billiard rooms created an opulence that contrasted sharply with the
congestion and filth of the city. Working-class saloons, fitted with substantial bars and a full complement of liquors, offered a respite from
the drudgery of the workplace and the limited comforts of cramped
apartments and cottages. The saloon was the workingman's club,
where he could enjoy the camaraderie of his friends from the job or the
neighborhood.[39]

American Victorian concepts of morality and respectability dictated
that while all men might fall prey to the baser appetites, good women,
as guardians of the home and of morality, were to remain pure. Thus

CLUB ROOM.
10

JAPANESE THRONE ROOM.
11

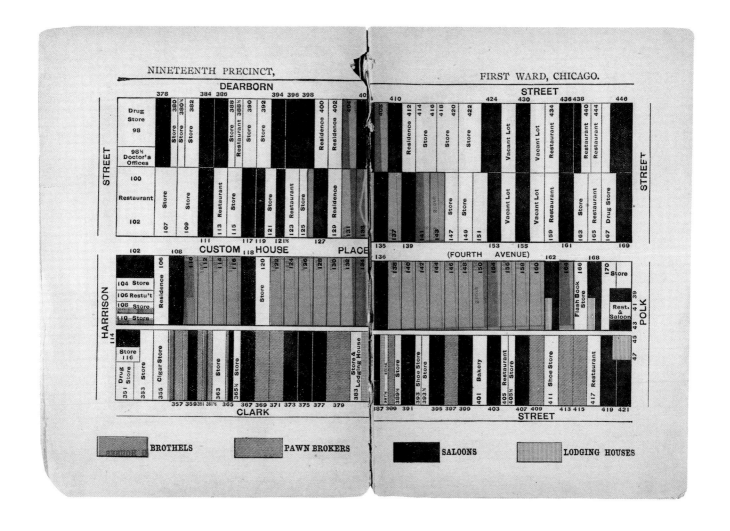

NINETEENTH PRECINCT,   FIRST WARD, CHICAGO.

BROTHELS   PAWN BROKERS   SALOONS   LODGING HOUSES

The neighborhood saloon—the workingman's club—allowed men to enjoy the companionship of friends. Boys often went to the saloons to find their fathers or to bring home "growlers" of beer for them.

many places of amusement were off-limits to her. Saloons were a male domain, but by the 1890s the beer garden had been accepted by non-Germans as a decent place for women.[40] Many women assumed active roles in enforcing the moral standards. While the saloon provided a convivial meeting place, it also fostered "the blight of drunkenness." Many temperance advocates were activated not only by religious or moral beliefs, but also by their concern for the effect of a man's drunkenness on his wife and children. Many of those who fought against prostitution did so to protect the numerous young girls tricked into prostitution by pimps or lured into it because of their poverty. In the 1890s the concern over vice in Chicago grew; it peaked in the following decade, reflecting the increased fears of parents for their children as those children left the confines of the ethnic communities and residential neighborhoods to look for fun in other parts of the city.

Although all groups had developed their institutional networks to maintain and to transmit to their children their religious, ethical, and cultural values, many young people looked outside the small worlds of their parents to the larger world of the city. In school and at work they often encountered young people from other groups, and they shared a common language. The promise of the city for excitement and personal fulfillment beckoned. As their parents had begun the transformation of personal life, leaving their larger kin networks and the farms and small towns, the children also broke new ground. Without the easy sociability of the small town and the arranged marriages of the old country, the young people of Chicago in the 1890s sought new ways to enjoy respectable leisure activities and meet a possible mate. Most workplaces were segregated by sex, and long hours left little time for socializing. While fraternal and social groups chaperoned dances once or twice a year and organized picnics in the summer, places for the young to meet and enjoy themselves were scarce in Chicago. As young people asked where the fun was, they too looked outside the neighborhood.

"THE BLIGHT OF DRUNKENNESS."

Chicagoans drank heavily by modern standards; temperance advocates believed that drinking harmed families. The Graphic, *1894.*

Work and Class

The best-known millionaires in Chicago were Marshall Field (above), Philip Armour (below), and George Pullman (facing page, above). Each was a self-made man who had built his fortune in creating a new industry.

While ethnic and racial groups created distinct communities in Chicago, the development of the economy also shaped the social fabric. Capitalizing on its position as the transportation link between the urban East and the agricultural Midwest, Chicago became not only a trade center but also an industrial center. Its major industries—steel making, railroad car building, meat packing, garment making, merchandising, agricultural implement manufacturing, and furniture making—ensured the city's place in the national economy. Chicagoans processed raw materials, made basic domestic goods for sale to the farms and small towns of America, and created the machinery—railroads, plows, and combines—that reaped, processed, and transported food for Americans. The vast expansion of industry in Chicago created jobs of every description and increased the demand for workers of all skills. Chicagoans did not, however, prosper equally. By the 1890s three distinct economic groups—wealthy capitalists, the middle class, and organized workers—were critical to the development of the city.

Nineteenth-century Americans, unlike most Americans today, were comfortable with the vocabulary of class. The self-employed proudly called themselves capitalists, and many of their employees, mostly blue-collar workers, proclaimed the worth of the working class. In the twentieth century the decline of self-employment among professionals and businesspeople and the increase in the number of managers and clerical workers has swelled the middle class. In the 1890s this process had only begun in Chicago and other cities. Seventy percent of all male heads of Chicago's households were blue-collar workers in 1900.[41] Although they were a minority of the population, the middle class of small businessmen, doctors, lawyers, salesmen, and clerks affected the city in the development of its residential neighborhoods. Through their buying power they also supported the commercial enterprises of the Loop. In the 1890s members of the middle class also articulated their vision for the city, one in their own image. They joined the attempts to mitigate the unprecedented unemployment between 1893 and 1897 and to arbitrate the conflict between big capitalists and organized workers in the Pullman Strike.[42]

The big capitalists were the smallest but most powerful economic group in Chicago in the 1890s—men like Marshall Field, Philip Armour, and George Pullman, who had made millions from the firms they founded. Their decisions shaped the lives of thousands of Chicagoans—their workers and the workers' families. Most led large and far-flung empires and had many financial interests in addition to the companies that bore their names. From his office in the Pullman Building on the corner of Michigan Avenue and Adams Street, George Pullman kept in touch with Pullman Company branches across the United States, Canada, and Mexico and invested his funds in new railroads and other businesses. Pullman sought to monopolize the sleeping-car business, and he was fast approaching his goal in the 1890s.[43] Others, like the Big Five meat packers, formed associations and divided the market among themselves. Competition was something to crush. The concentration of industry in the hands of a few continued throughout the 1890s as the number of manufacturing establishments in Chicago decreased by over two thousand while the number of manufacturing workers increased by over seventy thousand.[44] After they had reaped large profits from their initial endeavors, the big capitalists invested in each other's firms. By the 1890s they worked together, often serving on the boards of directors of each other's companies. Less competitors than partners, they combined in managing their empires and in projecting a vision for the city.

Although they were shrewd enough to reinvest much of their income, Chicago's big businessmen also spent money on a lavish scale. The city homes of the Pullmans, Armours, Fields, Palmers, Glessners, and others resembled European castles or chateaux, crammed full of the most costly furnishings and attended by large staffs of servants. Their wives

Chicago's millionaires spent their money at home, building mini-castles and chateaux. Pullman's Prairie Avenue mansion, 1887, was among Chicago's most elaborate.

Chicago's wealthiest citizens traveled to Europe often. Paris embodied their vision of a great city for, among other features, its planned boulevards such as the Champs-Elysées (right, 1907). In 1890 even smaller cities like Boston and Baltimore could boast of excellent universities, but Chicago lacked this manifestation of a great metropolis. Below: Harvard Yard looking north from Matthews Hall, 1892.

and daughters wore Paris originals and exquisite jewels, and they traveled within the city in fine horse-drawn carriages. Chicago's wealthiest citizens formed a social elite with a structured round of parties, dinners, and debuts. They could afford the finest entertainments—theater and concerts—that the city provided, but before the 1890s they were not able to enjoy the appurtenances of what they considered a great city unless they traveled to Paris, London, or New York.[45]

Wealthy Americans of the late nineteenth century frequently traveled abroad, and they viewed the European capitals as models of urban development. A great city had beautiful boulevards, fine buildings in a neo-classical style, museums, concert halls, universities, and lovely parks.[46] Such cities supported the fine arts as they defined them—music, painting, sculpture, and architecture. In 1890 Chicago had some lovely parks but precious little of the rest. Unlike Paris Chicago had had no Baron Haussmann to build great boulevards and integrate them with monuments and public buildings. For almost two decades Boston and New York had had good art museums, but Chicago had none, even though many wealthy Chicagoans had important private art collections. Chicago had an extraordinary new concert hall, the Auditorium, built in 1889, but no resident symphony to play in it. While Chicago was known for commerce, knowledge seemed to reside elsewhere, in Boston's Harvard University, New York's Columbia, or Baltimore's Johns Hopkins. In the 1890s Chicago's big capitalists decided to create the aspects of a great city that they thought their hometown lacked. Based on their experiences in building huge companies singlehandedly, Chicago's businessmen did not hesitate to spend large sums of money on cultural organizations on the basis of their own judgment.

The millionaires of the 1890s were typically self-made men; their ideas and business acumen had lifted them from modest circumstances to positions of unprecedented wealth. They trusted their own judgment and took large financial risks willingly. While this confidence enabled them to be forceful leaders, it also had negative consequences. The big capitalists created ever larger corporations, but they only slowly established the bureaucracies to manage them. As their companies grew, the leaders often retained the outlook of small businessmen who believed that they, and they alone, should make decisions. Although tens of thousands of employees, suppliers, and customers they did not know now depended on their company, they were reluctant to allow these people to contribute to, and hence possibly control, decision making. In the small firms of their youth, when the owner had known each employee, customer, and supplier, concrete knowledge of the needs and wishes of these people could affect an owner's decision. Those who now ran empires found it much more difficult to make decisions that included the needs or ideas of others. In the 1890s the labor conflicts created by this attitude would virtually tear the city apart.

Most Chicagoans were neither middle class nor big capitalists, but workers in the city's factories, stores, homes, offices, and streets. Men, women, and children had their own niches in the city's economy, and the niches rarely overlapped. Some men, though their numbers were declining, were skilled workers who made wages enough to support a family, purchase a worker's cottage, and enjoy a little amusement. Despite the promise of the city, however, many workers labored long hours for small wages and worried that sickness or unemployment might plunge their families into poverty. The great labor conflicts of the late nineteenth century emanated from the transformation of work through mass production methods, which eliminated or threatened the jobs of skilled workers and their standard of living.[47]

Skilled workers were the aristocrats of Chicago's working class; most Chicagoans had much less interesting or remunerative jobs. Every area of manufacturing needed some skilled workers, especially the thriving building trades. Some crafts, like baking and brewing, were declining in Chicago, but the need for machinists grew with the increased demand

Skilled furniture workers could command good wages and working conditions.

Carpenters tools, c. 1870. The hand tools of the skilled worker were still important in many industries in the 1890s, especially furniture making. [Plate 5]

Men in the construction trades could file liens on real estate, which could be enforced in court, to ensure payment of their wages. Mechanic's lien, 1892

to build and repair machine tools. The furniture-making industry, one of the city's largest, used many skilled workers such as carvers, cabinet-makers, and upholsterers.[48] German and Scandinavian immigrants who had learned woodworking in their youth entered the industry early, and their sons followed.

The skilled trades were men's work, and boys could learn them through formal apprenticeships. As a legal contract, an indenture bound a minor to work for several years; in return he would be taught a trade. The indenture made in 1902 between the father of William Lemme and Holmes, Pyott & Co. was for four years, during which William was to learn to be an iron molder.[49] The contract specified an increasing rate of pay for each year of the term. Like all workers of this period, however, William was not to be compensated for any sick time. William's wages, like those of all apprentices, were lower than those he might have earned in another job. At the end of his term, however, he would have a skill that commanded twice the wages of an unskilled laborer.

Skilled workers in America not only received relatively high wages, but they also had shorter hours and more control over their jobs than did other workers, who worked nine or ten hours a day, six days a week, and often faced seasonal layoffs with no assurance of being called back to work. Craftsmen only attained this position, however, because of continued pressure on their employers. In the building trades, for instance, workers frequently threatened legal action to collect their wages. Mechanics' liens and demands for wages were so common that standard printed forms were available. Skilled workers organized in trade unions to secure higher wage rates and better working conditions. The unions sought contracts with employers to specify the terms of work. In 1899 the Architectural Iron Workers' Union and the employers' organization, the Architectural Iron League, signed an agreement specifying an eight-

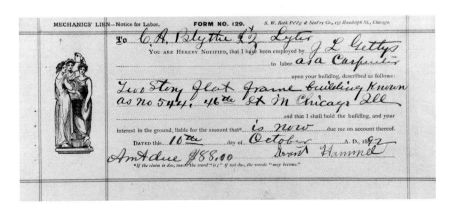

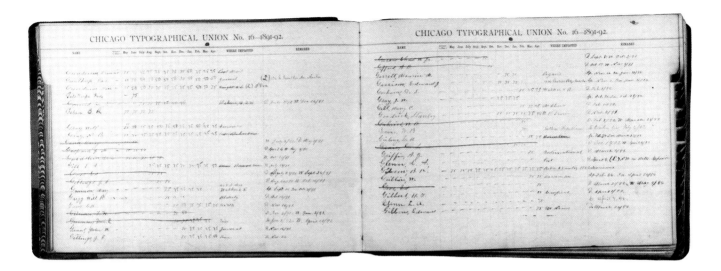

hour day, with a half-day on Saturday and a minimum wage of thirty-seven-and-a-half cents per hour and overtime pay.[50] Workers in the nineteenth century were often paid in store orders or scrip; the union agreement demanded currency.

To protect the jobs of skilled workers, the agreement also specified the ratio of apprentices to journeymen. Employers often paid apprentices very low wages and hired fewer skilled workers. The contract ensured the continuation of the union by specifying a closed shop—employers agreed not to hire anyone who was not a union member. It further allowed the union to engage in sympathy strikes, honoring the picket lines of other unions that called strikes. Through the joint action of the many craft unions in the building trades, individual unions gained the power to make favorable contracts. Unions collected weekly or monthly dues to build their funds, which supported members during strikes and provided unemployment, health, or death benefits.

Although skilled workers were still in demand in the 1890s, mass production became the key to the growth of Chicago's industries. Mass production meant using more machines and laborers with fewer skills to cut costs and boost productivity. Many of Chicago's furniture makers, for instance, mechanized production, favoring a cheaper grade of mass-produced goods over the high-quality, handmade ones. The slogan of the Chicago Cottage Organ Company, "One Organ Every 10 Minutes. 60 Organs Per Day. 18,000 Organs Per Year," exemplified the trend. The expansion in the number of semiskilled and unskilled jobs provided opportunities for new Chicagoans from rural backgrounds who had no training as artisans.

Membership roll, Chicago Typographical Union No. 16, 1891–92. The key to the success of the craft union was collecting dues regularly so that the union could sustain strikes and pay members during unemployment and illness.

The Chicago Cottage Organ Co. boasted of its speed in manufacturing organs in 1893. Mass production was the wave of the future in all industries.

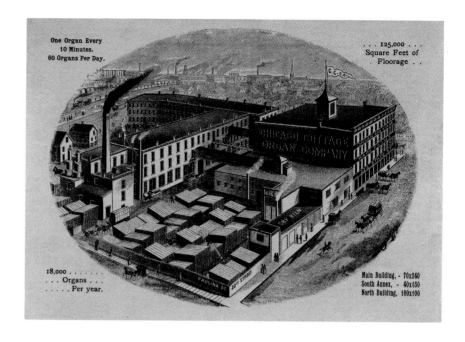

The meat-packing industry perfected the most advanced techniques of mass production in Chicago. Although the process was not highly mechanized, the companies devised a microscopic division of labor. The killing gang of 157 men, for instance, was divided into 78 "trades." The overhead rail that pulled the carcasses along created an assembly-line-like operation in which each man repeated his task throughout the day.[51] Separate departments handled each step in the process, and thousands of animals could be processed each day. Such innovations in the production process made Chicago the country's meat-packing center and allowed the Big Five companies (Armour, Swift, Nelson Morris, Continental Packing Co., and Libby, McNeill & Libby Co.) to drive out the competition of traditional local butchers.

These jobs, which could be learned in a few days or weeks, presented opportunities for the newest and least skilled immigrants to Chicago. Those who had only farm experience or who spoke no English could do these jobs with little difficulty. By the 1890s Poles, Lithuanians, and other eastern Europeans flooded into the meat-packing industry on the lowest levels. The few skilled workers in the industry usually came from the older immigrant groups like the Irish, Germans, or Bohemians. The immigrants formed a vast labor pool for employers to draw on as they expanded production; businessmen saw the young and unskilled as an asset to the city, not a problem. This need controlled the nativist surge

TRIMMING.

Left: Working conditions in the meat pack-ing plants were disgusting; blood covered everything and the stench was overpowering. Below: the butcher's traditional block and cleaver (c. 1900) were becoming an anach-ronism throughout America as Chicago's mass-produced meat was shipped throughout the United States.

of the 1890s. Although immigration created cultural conflicts, business-men generally remained staunch supporters of open immigration and promoted a certain degree of toleration.

Because they were so easily replaced, however, the new packing-house workers had little leverage with their employers. The semiskilled and unskilled bore the brunt of low wages, long hours, instability of employ-ment, and layoffs. To find work, men had to report early each morning but might not be employed for several hours. Then they might work until ten at night or for only a few hours. Regardless of how long they waited, they were paid only for the hours they actually worked. The next day they would repeat this process. Men made as little as fifteen cents per hour, and nine to ten dollars per week was a typical wage.

The accident rate posed a serious problem in meat packing. The pace was cruel, and accidents were frequent. Safety equipment was not found in Chicago's factories, but some industries—meat packing, steel making, railroad passenger car construction—were much more hazardous than others. When the state of Illinois began keeping industrial accident sta-tistics in 1907, 99 workers were killed and 428 injured in Chicago in a six-month period.[52] In an era before either workmen's compensation or social security, these accidents threatened whole families with poverty as the chief breadwinner's earnings disappeared.

Working conditions in many industries also caused health problems. The appalling conditions that Upton Sinclair recounted in his 1906 best-

The specialization of labor was extensive in meat packing; trimming was one of many tasks repeated endlessly. Photograph by Adolph Witteman, 1892.

HEADS OFF.

seller, *The Jungle*, resulted from investigations of Chicago's meat-packing plants in the 1890s. Sinclair exposed the fearful toll that the production process took on the new immigrant workers:

Then, too, a still more dreadful thing happened to him; he worked in a place where his feet were soaked in chemicals, and it was not long before they had eaten through his new boots. Then sores began to break out on his feet, and grow worse and worse. Whether it was that his blood was bad, or there had been a cut, he could not say; but he asked the men about it, and learned that it was a regular thing—it was the saltpetre. Every one felt it, sooner or later, and then it was all up with him, at least for that sort of work. The sores would never heal—in the end his toes would drop off, if he did not quit.[53]

While the meat-packing plants were among the worst work environments, the typical small factory left much to be desired. Even if the factory was not hazardous, it was often unpleasant. Most had dingy lighting, dirty windows, and littered floors. The machines and the workers were crowded together, and there was no place to wash or to eat lunch except among the machinery. Toilet facilities were dirty, and a bucket of water often passed for the water fountain. The machines clattered and

Table 7—Fatal Accidents—Continued.

Manufacturers —Continued.

ILLINOIS STEEL CO.—CHICAGO.

1907.		Name of Killed	Age.	Occupation.	Place of Residence.	Nativity.	Married.	Single.	Cause of Death.
July	23	A. Biroczak	40	Laborer..............	Chicago	Pole......................		1	Gas, overcome by ....
	26	J. Fignonta	30	Weighman..............	..do..............	..do..............	1		Railroad car and stock pocket...... ......
August	1	Wm. Totten..............	28	Electrician	..do..............	American	1		Crane and wall ....
	1	Parr Traska..............	23	Laborer..............	..do..............	Russian		1	Falling controller ....
	5	John Erickson	32	Sailor..............	..do..............	Swede..............		1	Electric current ....
	25	George Boguaslaski	28	Switchman	..do..............	Pole..............	1		Falling mould ....
	1	S. Bartomey	40	Hooker..............	..do..............	..do..............		1	Falling angles......................
October	8	Frank Jankoski..............	36	Laborer..............	..do..............	..do..............		1	Falling iron ....
	24	Peter Gorda..............	22	..do..............	Joliet	Italian		1	Flying hot metal ....
	30	G. Radancic..............	24	..do..............	Chicago	Austrian	1		Fell into ore pocket ....
November	19	Andrew Miclea..............	21	..do..............	Joliet	Roumanian		1	Fell from hoist ....
December	1	Joseph Krelak	36	Machinist..............	Chicago	Pole......................		1	Frame and rail runway ....
	3	John Behrens	26	Craneman..............	..do..............	American		1	Flying hot metal ....

Bureau of Labor Statistics, First Report on Industrial Accidents in Illinois for the Six Months Ending December 31, 1907, *1908. The industrial accident rate was very high in certain industries—steel making, meat packing, and railroad car construction were especially dangerous. Left: Laundry, c. 1890. Many workplaces were crowded, damp, dingy, and noisy.*

rattled loudly. Where chemicals or natural products produced disgusting smells, the workplace was repulsive.

In his novel *Sister Carrie,* Theodore Dreiser described the physical toll of the repetitive machine tasks in a shoe factory:

Her hands began to ache at the wrists and then in the fingers, and towards the last she seemed one mass of dull, complaining muscles, fixed in an eternal position and performing a single mechanical movement which became more and more distasteful, until at last it was absolutely nauseating.[54]

Construction of old Tribune Building, Dearborn and Madison streets, 1901. The unskilled labor of digging, hauling, and pushing a broom was still in great demand in Chicago in the 1890s.

Because employers did not provide seats, most machine tenders were forced to stand. The resulting fatigue and swelling legs and feet were part of the job. Workers maintained productivity because they feared the foremen, who could fire at will. Many foremen drove the workers with screams and curses and sometimes with blows.

Although factory jobs varied greatly in desirability, the bottom of the occupational ladder was not the newly created semiskilled jobs, but the unskilled labor of pushing a broom, hauling, and digging. Laborers were everywhere in the streets of Chicago, digging the sewers and underground utilities, the foundations for new buildings, and the beds for the railroads that crisscrossed the city. They were paid by the day for jobs that lasted only a day or two. Then the laborers had to look elsewhere for work. Facing frequent spells of unemployment, they had the most precarious existence of all the adult workers in the city. In 1900 over seventy-five thousand people—or 10 percent of all workers in the city—were unskilled laborers, constituting the single largest occupational category.[55]

While many laborers were permanent residents of the city, a large number were transients. As the rail center of the nation, Chicago was the home base for a huge army of migrant workers who picked crops, built railroads, worked in sawmills, and performed the other seasonal, outdoor tasks. These men had few resources and stayed near the employment agents and the rail yards. They lived in the lodging houses if they were not homeless. An 1899 survey by John Bogue showed that ten thousand men bunked each night in the city's seventy-five lodging houses, which provided a cot, but rarely clean sheets, for ten to twenty-five cents per night.[56]

If men found a great range of jobs in Chicago in the 1890s, women's choices were limited. Only one in five Chicago workers was a woman. Most Americans believed that husbands should be the breadwinners for their families and that wives should take care of the house and the children. Only the poorest married women worked for wages. Working-class families expected, however, that daughters, like sons, would contribute to family finances, and most of the women in Chicago who worked for wages were young, single girls. Although a few daughters of the middle class explored careers in the 1890s, the idea that housekeeping and childrearing were a woman's primary task governed women's

As many as ten thousand men bunked each night in the city's seventy-five cheap lodging houses. Drawing by Charles Mente, Harper's Weekly, *c. 1894.*

Most women who worked did so as maids in private homes or as laundresses. The long hours and low status made those jobs undesirable.

work throughout the city. The only substantial number of middle-class jobs for women were in teaching. Some new jobs, like typing, stenography, and department store sales, were opening up for women. Most jobs, however, remained men's work, and women would not be hired for them, if they applied. Women's wages were set on a lower level than men's, and most women felt lucky to make as much as an unskilled male laborer.

Many Chicago women worked at garment making, often in sweatshop conditions. In the garment industry, as in most factory work that was open to them, women were usually paid for each completed piece, not for time worked. While men often made hourly or daily wages, women's wages were more likely to be tied directly to productivity. Piece rates encouraged each woman to work as fast as she possibly could to earn a living wage. A schedule of rates demanded by the glovemakers union in 1905 shows the incredibly low rates that led to overwork: one demand was for four cents to sew a dozen pair of small mittens.[57] In the diary she kept as a twenty-year-old glovemaker, Agnes Nestor recorded her frequent fatigue and her dismay on "Blue Monday."[58] This was the term in common use among workers in semiskilled and unskilled jobs who dreaded going back to them after a day of rest. In 1893 Chicagoan Florence Kelley fought for a state law to limit women's employment to eight hours a day, but the law was struck down by the Illinois Supreme Court. The Illinois Association of Manufacturers continued to fight any restriction on women's hours.[59]

The largest group of women workers did not labor in industry, however; they worked for wages as servants and laundresses. More than a quarter of Chicago's working women held these jobs, and most worked in homes, not laundries or hotels.[60] Most women were trained as young girls to perform this work in anticipation of their future role as wives and mothers. Because live-in servants received room and board, their wages usually equaled those of factory workers. Their hours, however, were much longer; the servant was on call up to eighteen hours per day, seven days a week. The living arrangements were isolating, as a woman rarely saw friends or family. The greatest drawback to domestic service, however, was its low status. Americans viewed service as demeaning and associated it with slavery or the class system of Europe. Many white women were servants, but increasingly girls chose factory work with its shorter hours and greater prestige. Black women had almost no opportunities outside of domestic service, and in the twentieth century they became the majority of Chicago's servants.[61]

my outs so we had to walk about a mile in the hot sun. But then we had a good time when we got there. We arived home about six o'clock good and hungry. In the evening we sat out front and watched the fire-works.

5 I stayed home all evening.

6 Nothing of any import- ance happened today.

7 I am so dissapointed tonight that I can

hardly write. We re- ceived a letter today from the Caren girls saying they cannot come this summer. We went down to North Av. and got some white collars.

8 I wrote a letter to Arthur. This evening we took a walk.

9 This is Blue Monday. Tonight we went down to North Av. and when we came back went for a walk with Mrs. Faber.

Agnes Nestor recorded the fatigue of sweat- shop labor in her diary in 1900 (left), when she was twenty years old.

Below: Sweatshop inspection, 1903. The gar- ment trade was one of the few industries in which many women were hired.

Margaret Haley (above) was president of the Chicago Teachers Federation, the first teachers' union, formed in 1897. Below: The Chicago Teachers Federation made its case for higher wages by comparing Chicago's pay scale with that of New York in 1899.

Women also became more assertive in other job situations in the 1890s. Chicago's public school teachers, most of whom were women from working-class backgrounds, formed the first union of teachers, the Chicago Teachers Federation (CTF), in 1897. Margaret Haley served as its president for most of its thirty active years. The CTF fought to protect teachers' tenure rights and their wages.[62]

Given the low wages of many of Chicago's adults and the instability of their employment, it was inevitable that many children would have to work. Contemporaries defined child labor as wage work by children under the age of fourteen. Before a high school education was necessary for most jobs, many young people, including the sons of the middle class, held jobs. Boys who looked forward to an office job often began work between the ages of twelve and fourteen as messengers or junior clerks. According to Chicago's school census for 1894, almost seven thousand children between the ages of seven and fourteen did not attend any school.[63] The state outlawed the labor of children under fourteen in factories, but the law was widely flouted, especially in the garment industry and the stockyards. It would have taken an army of factory inspectors to check on all the sweatshops, and parents colluded with employers to break the law if the family needed money. These children not only failed to get an education, but they were subjected to the same

TEACHERS' SALARIES.

ELEMENTARY SCHOOLS.

NEW YORK.			CHICAGO.		
	PRIMARY.	GRAMMAR.		PRIMARY.	GRAMMAR.
1st Year	$ 600	$ 600	1st Year	$ 500	$ 500
4th "	720	720	4th "	650	675
7th "	825	825	7th "	800	825
9th "	1056	1056	8th "	875	900
11th "	1188	1188	9th "	(Schedule.) * 925	(Schedule.) * 950
13th "	1320	1320	10th "	(Schedule.) * 975	(Schedule.) *1000
16th "	1380	1380	11th "	(Schedule.) *1000	(Schedule.) *1000

* Salaries for 9th, 10th and 11th years adopted by Board of Education, March 9th, 1898, and schedule suspended for fiscal year of 1899.

conditions that caused so many industrial accidents and occupational diseases among adults.

While many Chicagoans sought the power of the state to abolish child labor, others tried to help children get jobs if the family needed money. With no public welfare for mothers whose husbands had died or deserted them, women could rarely support their children alone. Numerous orphanages existed to take the "half-orphans," as the children of

TRY, O TRY.

AIR—" Buy a Broom."

O, stitching is witching
  And hemming as well,
But what is distressing
  Is turning a fell.
I'm sick of such seaming,
  And ready to cry,
But I hear the word ringing.
  "Try. little one, try,
Try, O try; try, O try:"
  I hear the word ringing,
" Try, little one, try."

And so I am striving
  As hard as can be
To keep back from crying,
  Just so I can see.
And may be with helping
  At last I shall learn
The worst fringy edges
  Most neatly to turn.
" Try, O try; try, O try;"
  I hear. etc.

Above: This flyer of industrial school songs, c. 1890, from the South Side Tabernacle was used to teach tasks to daughters of the poor so that they could support themselves as domestic servants.

Left: Newsboys often lived as well as worked on the streets.

Child labor was sometimes unavoidable; some parents made low wages, and no welfare programs existed to help mothers who had been widowed or abandoned. Right: The Chicago Waifs' Mission and Training School helped train, place, and house working children. Many children found work on the streets shining shoes (below). Illustration by J. G. Brown, The Graphic, 1893.

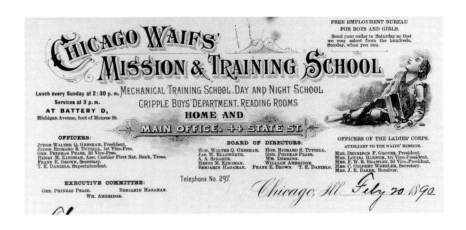

these women were known. Rather than surrender their children to institutions, many mothers tried to find work for all their children. Some religious groups provided training and guidance for child laborers. The South Side Tabernacle's Industrial School taught housekeeping and sewing to girls. The Industrial School Songbook had a song for every task: "Shopping Song," "The Washing Song," "Fasten the Thread," "The Dusting Song," and "Try, O Try."[64] The Chicago Waifs' Mission and Training School provided a home for forty to fifty boys, as well as day and night classes, reading rooms, and a "cripple boys' department."[65] It advertised for employers to "send your order in Saturday so that we may select from the hundreds [of children], Sunday."

The state's first factory inspector, Florence Kelley, detailed the exploitation of children in the factories and drew attention to the number of children working in unregulated sectors of the economy:

In considering the need of further protective legislation for working children, the fact should not be lost sight of that they are flocking into occupations wholly without legal restriction. Among children found in unregulated employments are newsboys and newsgirls, bootblacks, street peddlers, office boys, telegraph and messenger boys, laundry girls, and children in mercantile occupations.[66]

These children worked at all hours of the day and night, in all weather, and, like those who worked in factories, they made only a pittance. Many lived as well as worked on the streets.

Civic Crises at Mid-Decade

The economic system created two problems—unemployment and labor conflict—that reached crisis proportions in the 1890s. While neither was resolved by a unified civic response, they prompted the creation of new

CENTRAL YARD:
Superior and Roberts Sts.
Telephone N. 415.

SOUTH SIDE YARD:
34th St. and Armour Ave.
Telephone S. 256.

THE CHICAGO RELIEF AND AID SOCIETY

Respectfully requests your patronage for their Woodyards.

The object of the yards is to give employment to such distressed able-bodied men as are known, through investigation, to be worthy of help.

Last year we gave work at our North and West side yards to 4931 men, who fully appreciated the chance to earn a dollar when all other sources of employment were closed to them.

In giving work to such a number we accumulate an immense stock of sawed wood, which we must sell to continue the good work. The more wood we sell the more work we can give. We have

KINDLING, SLABS, HICKORY, MAPLE AND OAK

in lengths suitable for stove, grate, fireplace or furnace, and of the best quality. We guarantee quantity and price to be just and satisfactory.

Will you not help us without additional expense to yourself by buying our wood at the regular market price?—and kindly speak of us to your friends.

J. M. WANZER, Chairman,
Z. R. CARTER, } Committee on Woodyards.
ROBERT M. WELLS,

Chicagoans expected each able-bodied man to take care of himself and his family, and they suspected the unemployed of laziness. The wood yard operated by the Chicago Relief and Aid Society was intended to employ the worthy. Engraving by Benedict & Co., 1896–1900.

citywide coalitions and attempts to define civic responsibility more broadly than it had been in previous decades.

Despite burgeoning industrial development, unemployment ran high in the city even in the best years. In an era before unemployment insurance, the loss of a job meant poverty and often homelessness for

In If Christ Came to Chicago *(1894), William Stead excoriated Chicagoans for worshiping money and ignoring their responsibility for the less fortunate.*

working-class families. Unions frequently offered unemployment benefits to members, but most of Chicago's workers did not belong to unions. Private philanthropy was directed at those who were deemed worthy: widows, orphans, the blind, and the handicapped. Every able-bodied adult male was expected to find a job. If he failed and his family suffered, others considered him at fault. The Chicago Relief and Aid Society sponsored two wood yards to employ only "such distressed able-bodied men as are known, through investigation, to be worthy of help."[67] As in most large cities, Chicago's police stations regularly sheltered the homeless

The total number of meals furnished from our three kitchens was 462,084
The average per day was.. 4,621
Total number of working days............................... 83
Average number per day.................................. 2,275
Largest number on any one day, exclusive of married men in
   7th, 8th and 19th wards. (See page 21) 3,760
Daily average of hours 8,582
Average hours per man per day.................3 hours and 35 minutes
Total lodging checks issued to regular lodging houses......... 232,066
Total days on which lodgings were issued.................... 94
Total orders on warehouse for family supplies................ 8,682
Value of the supplies.......................................$3,551.60

The articles of clothing issued were as follows :

2,473 Pairs shoes.   19 Coats.
4,236 Pairs of socks.   16 Vests.
3,576 Pairs of mittens.   5 Overcoats.
2,160 Pieces underwear.   9 Shirts.
  425 Caps.   3 Trusses.
1,151 Pairs trousers.   1 Elastic stocking.
14,074 articles costing.......................................$6,324.71
    60 dozen mittens (donated), value 54.00
             Total value $6,378.71

In the winter of 1893–94, the newly formed Civic Federation sought to cope with unemployment by setting up the Central Relief Association to coordinate and augment the services available for the poor.

by offering them a bare floor and sometimes a beating. Chicago police stations housed over thirty thousand homeless men during the relatively prosperous year of 1890.[68]

During the depression years of 1893 to 1897, unemployment reached record levels in Chicago and the country. Men, women, and children scoured the garbage dumps for food, and the mayor allowed the homeless to sleep in City Hall as well as the police stations.[69] The traditional methods of charity, however, could not alleviate the suffering. In 1893 English journalist William Stead came to Chicago to attend the world's fair. What he saw in the "gray city" rather than the "white city" appalled him. In a series of mass meetings he sought to awaken Chicagoans to the corruption and inhumanity of the city. He charged Chicagoans with the sin of greed, of worshiping the new trinity of Marshall Field, George Pullman, and Philip Armour, and of having forgotten the message of the New Testament.[70] In response, a group of forty civic leaders (including Field) joined together to form the Civic Federation to concentrate "into one potential, non-political, non-sectarian center . . . all the forces that are now laboring to advance our municipal, philanthropic, industrial and moral interests, and to accomplish all that is possible towards energizing and giving effect to the public conscience of Chicago."[71] The federation

Jane Addams (above) and Graham Taylor (below), leaders of the new social reform movement coming out of the social settlements, joined businessmen and others to form the Civic Federation.

brought together businessmen, philanthropists, labor leaders, reformers, educators, religious leaders, and representatives of some of the ethnic communities. This diverse gathering signaled the realization that the problems of the city necessitated a larger civic consciousness.

The Civic Federation created task forces on philanthropy, moral reform, industry, education, and legislation; its first activity was to form the Central Relief Association to coordinate the relief effort during the worst winter of the depression. For the first time since the Great Fire of 1871, a citywide effort was made to ease suffering. No such effort had been made in the depression years of the mid-1870s. The Civic Federation's policy signified a new recognition that the industrial economy and not merely individual inadequacy caused unemployment.[72] The Central Relief Association raised $135,000 and coordinated the provision of almost half a million meals furnished at soup kitchens, a quarter of a million lodgings for the homeless, and thousands of jobs for unemployed men. The Central Relief Association evolved over the next two decades into the United Charities, the central coordinating body for Chicago's private social service agencies. Chicagoans recognized that poverty and need were endemic and had to be continually addressed.[73]

Among the first members of the Civic Federation were Jane Addams and Graham Taylor, leaders of a new generation of social reformers who inspired the Progressive movement of the twentieth century. The social reformers were children of neither wealthy capitalists nor the immigrant poor. They had grown up in middle-class comfort and became critics of the inhumanity of the big cities. Addams, Taylor, and others saw the immigrant poor used and abused by the great industries in Chicago and then left to fend for themselves in adversity. They saw urban life and poverty severely strain family relations, and they sought to keep children from delinquency and to help the child whose parents were cruel or neglectful. In the 1890s reformers like Taylor and Addams investigated the life of the poor in Chicago and began to effect solutions. Although they did much on the level of private charity, they began to agitate for a governmental—or public—role in the solution of urban problems. Within a decade they had persuaded enough Americans of the usefulness of this course that they had created a new political movement—Progressivism.[74]

The activities of Civic Federation members and social reformers highlighted the importance of labor problems in Chicago in the 1890s, but they did not solve them. Industrial work in general created class conflict, and Chicago had been a center of labor union organizing and radical politics for decades. The Haymarket bombing in 1886, the subsequent

Left: The social reformers were especially concerned about the impact of slum life on children. Such children had no place to play and were easily led into delinquency.

Below: To keep wages high, trade unions sought to force each employer to pay standard wages. Wage scale of the German Waiters and Bartenders Association, 1890.

panic and massive repression of civil liberties, and the execution of the anarchist leaders exacerbated class hatred.[75] The Knights of Labor, which had led the movement for the eight-hour workday in 1886, still had many adherents in Chicago in the early 1890s. Chicago also had a large number of craft unions, such as the German Waiters and Bartenders Columbia Association; many such unions were chartered by the American Federation of Labor. These unions engaged in frequent strikes in the early 1890s to enforce their demands for wages and better working conditions.

Many spontaneous strikes occurred in industries without unions, such as the garment trade. No businesses had formal grievance or negotiating procedures, and when wages changed or problems arose, workers struck immediately to force employers to talk.[76] These strikes were ubiquitous before the age of formal procedures. If foremen had the power to make changes in wages or working conditions, such strikes were often settled in a few hours. When foremen did not have the power to make changes, the strikes lasted much longer. Distant employers often refused to rethink their decisions. A common response was to lock out the striking workers and bring in others who would accept the employer's terms. These problems of authority in industry came to a head in Chicago and the nation in the 1894 Pullman Strike.

The town of Pullman was a world-famous example of community planning; it won many awards and words of praise.

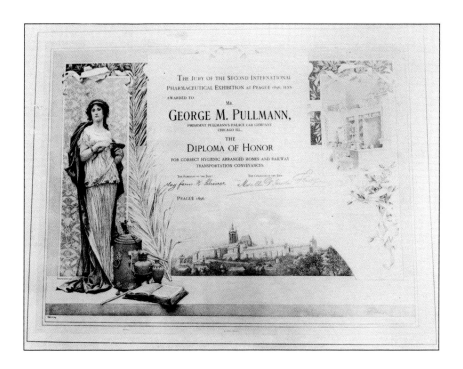

George Pullman had become one of the most famous Chicagoans not only because of his luxurious sleeping cars, but also because of his model town.[77] He built the town of Pullman in 1881 along with his new factory, the Pullman Car Works, at the south end of Hyde Park Township. With its brick housing, flower beds, and clean streets, the town of Pullman was admired by visitors from around the country and the world. It became one of Chicago's premier tourist attractions. Pullman had built the town to attract and increase the efficiency of the skilled workers he needed to build his sleeping cars. He believed that favorable neighborhood and home life would create better workers. So the town of Pullman had athletic facilities, a library, a theater, schools, and no saloons. To maintain the housing in the manner that he thought conducive to a good environment, Pullman would only rent to his workers, fearing they would change the housing if they owned it. He kept total control of the town's facilities, even after it was incorporated into Chicago with the rest of Hyde Park. The earliest criticisms of the town centered on this lack of democracy; Pullman was often considered a tyrant.

Pullman had put much thought into the town, but like most industrialists of the time, he was much less inventive within the factory. The same conditions that caused worker discontent elsewhere also existed in the Pullman Car Works: pay levels fluctuated greatly, piece rates were introduced, skilled jobs were being transformed into semiskilled ones,

Left: The clean, pleasant, tree-lined streets of Pullman contrasted starkly with the working-class slums of Chicago. View west on 112th Street from Market Hall.

and foremen disciplined harshly and played favorites. Although Pullman had expected his environmental approach would alleviate labor discontent, his workers joined the Knights of Labor and struck for the eight-hour day in 1886, and many small strikes erupted throughout the 1880s and early 1890s. In 1893, as the depression hit the Pullman Company, Pullman laid off many workers and slashed wage rates an average of 28 percent.[78]

Above: During the depression of 1893–97, when Pullman slashed wages but not rents, some workers took home only pennies for weeks of work. Paycheck to O. Millett for second half of August 1893.

In building his workers' paradise, Pullman had created the expectation that workers would get a better or a fairer deal from him than from other employers. In 1893 Pullman's workers were restive not simply because of the pay cuts and layoffs, but because of what they perceived as the company's lack of fairness. At the same time that workers suffered financially, management took no pay cuts, and the usual 8 percent dividend was paid to stockholders. Furthermore, Pullman refused to lower the rents on company housing. According to Pullman, rents in the model town had always been higher than those outside because of the town's higher quality. In the depression, however, workers could not pay such rents. As the company continued to deduct rent and utilities from paychecks, men like wood machinist O. Millett took home twelve cents for half a month's work.

In the winter of 1893–94, the Pullman workers organized and joined a new union, the American Railway Union.[79] The trend to concentration in business affected the railroads as it had the manufacturing industries, and a small number of railroads controlled the industry. Railway leaders

Pullman's workers flocked to join the new American Railway Union, led by Eugene Debs (above), in 1893. Photograph by Bundy, 1908. When the American Railway Union declared a boycott of trains carrying Pullman cars, the national press portrayed Debs as a dangerous dictator who controlled the fate of a nation dependent on rail transport (right). Facing page: The Pullman Palace Car Works.

KING DEBS.

formed the General Managers Association, headquartered in Chicago, to coordinate labor and pricing policies. The American Railway Union (ARU) was the first attempt by American workers to meet their employers on the national and industrywide level on which the employers had organized. Everyone who worked for a railroad could join the union, and its goal was a uniform contract with each railroad for all its workers. Eugene Debs headed the ARU, and by the spring of 1894 its membership had grown to 150,000. Many of Chicago's railroad workers joined along with the workers who made George Pullman's sleeping cars.

In May 1894 the Pullman workers brought their grievances to the company but got no satisfaction. After management fired three of their leaders, the workers called the strike. The Pullman Company, following its usual policy, locked out all the workers and waited for them to give in. The workers organized a relief fund and attempted to negotiate with the company, but they found the company unwilling to talk. Many Chicagoans of all classes agreed that the Pullman workers had just grievances and that they had conducted themselves responsibly during the

More than fourteen thousand troops, marshals, and police were stationed in Chicago to keep the trains moving, by force if necessary.

first month of the strike. The Civic Federation tried to arbitrate the strike. Although the workers agreed to talk, Pullman would not. Bertha Palmer, as vice president of the federation, tried to convince a Pullman director that the company had been "grasping or oppressive in their measures."[80] Civic Federation leaders learned, however, the limits of a voluntary local organization. Although Marshall Field was a member of the federation and a director of the Pullman Company, he refused to use his position on the board to change the company's stance.

One month into the strike, the ARU held its first annual meeting in Chicago, and the Pullman strikers asked the union for help. The ARU organized a boycott of all trains that included Pullman sleepers. What began as a quiet local strike became a national railroad strike. The General Managers Association took the opportunity to destroy the ARU before it became a real threat to the total management control they were used to. Although the American Railway Union made every effort to avoid interfering with the mails and to curb violence, the General Managers Association persuaded President Cleveland that the strike was a threat to the nation. The attorney general, who sat on the boards of directors of two railroads, secured an injunction against the union based on the Sherman Anti-Trust Act, making any attempt by union officials to continue the strike, such as speeches and communications, illegal. Debs and the rest of the union leadership were jailed when they refused to call off the strike. Although Governor Altgeld insisted that police and Illinois militia had the situation in hand and that there was little violence, the president listened to the desires of businessmen and ordered troops to Chicago and other areas. As the strike became a confrontation between the workers and the government, violence broke out in rail yards throughout the country, but especially near the stockyards in Chicago. At the height of the strike over fourteen thousand troops, marshals, and police were on duty in Chicago. Over one thousand rail cars were destroyed in Chicago alone, and thirteen people died in rioting.

When the violence abated, the railway union had been crushed and the strike was over. Pullman reopened the Car Works with eight hundred new workers and hired about two thousand former workers who swore to stay away from unions. Although Pullman won the strike, he was probably the most hated man not only in the town of Pullman but in Chicago. The strike bitterly divided workers and employers, and Pullman's name was an anathema in union circles for decades.

The strike encouraged two different responses among Chicago's workers. Skilled workers were drawn to the craft unions of the American

Despite protests from Governor Altgeld and Mayor Hopkins that there was no substantial violence, President Cleveland was persuaded to send federal troops to Chicago to break the strike. After federal troops arrived, violence escalated. More than one thousand rail cars were destroyed, and thirteen people died. Harper's Weekly, 1894.

Chicago's businessmen and railroad executives pressured for federal intervention. This telegram was sent on July 19, 1894, from Paul Morton to his father, Secretary of Agriculture J. Sterling Morton.

Federation of Labor, which took an ever dimmer view of industrywide organizing and concentrated on perfecting the solidarity of individual crafts. A new socialist movement also blossomed among those who believed that labor needed political control in addition to unions. In the 1880s Chicago's socialist and anarchist movements had been confined primarily to Germans and other immigrant groups. In the late 1890s a new American socialist movement formed under the leadership of Eugene Debs, who was converted to socialism while jailed for his strike leadership.[81] Chicago became a center of the new socialist movement, as

The socialist movement grew in the late 1890s as Chicagoans looked for ways to improve their lives. Charles Kerr published the Pocket Library of Socialism to promote the principles of socialism.

men like Clarence Darrow and Henry Demarest Lloyd voiced the socialists' new answers to many of the pressing issues of life in the city. The socialists advocated, for instance, municipal ownership of public utilities and health and safety laws for the workplace. Chicago's Kerr Publishing Company was the leading source of educational literature for this movement, and its Pocket Library of Socialism provided basic texts for five and ten cents each.

Reformer Jane Addams spoke for those who were appalled by the conduct of the strike and by Pullman's unwillingness to compromise in particular. In a speech after the strike, she called Pullman "the Modern Lear," a man who thought only he knew what was best and so brought tragedy to all.[82] In the years after the strike, many who were concerned about the costs of labor conflict on the social fabric would encourage the concept of arbitration, which the Civic Federation had proposed. The presidential commission appointed in the aftermath of the bloody strike to investigate its causes and conduct also supported the concept of arbitration; its report was the basis for future government regulation of labor relations in the railroad industry.[83] In a series of increasingly restrictive laws, Congress recognized the right of railroad workers to join unions but also mandated mediation and arbitration to avoid strikes. In the Pullman Strike and other strikes in the late nineteenth century, the government used its forces to help management win. After the Pullman Strike increasing numbers of political and civic leaders used government powers for conciliation. They expected both sides to compromise rather than to risk tearing society apart with class warfare.

The City Comes of Age

Although Chicagoans were divided by ethnicity, race, and class in the 1890s and the relations between them were often contentious, the decade was one of building, not of deterioration. As people who had come to Chicago with visions of something better, they shared a critical stance toward the city. Their very energy in migrating and building new industries, neighborhoods, and community organizations was a resource for the solution of urban problems. They would attack many of these problems as they had their personal dreams—by joining other individuals to form private organizations. As they began to define problems that required citywide solutions, however, Chicagoans also began to look for ways to create the coalitions that could achieve those solutions. For this they drew on their model of cooperation and tolerance, found first in the Civic Federation. The steps they made toward united efforts were the hardest, but the most important.

CHICAGO

OF TO-DAY

The METROPOLIS OF THE WEST.

2

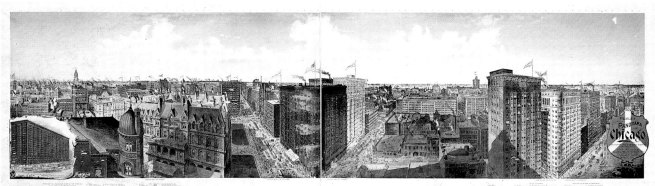

3

4

5

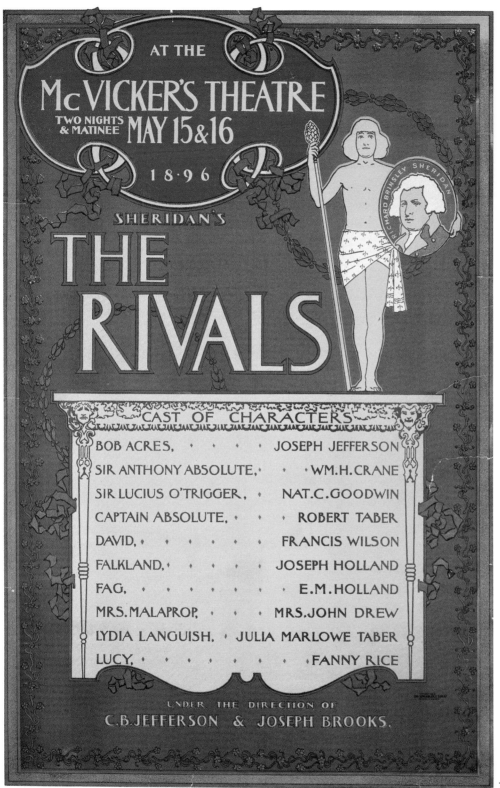

AT THE

Mc VICKER'S THEATRE

TWO NIGHTS & MATINEE **MAY 15 & 16**

1·8·96

SHERIDAN'S

THE RIVALS

RICHARD BRINSLEY SHERIDAN

CAST OF CHARACTERS

BOB ACRES,	JOSEPH JEFFERSON
SIR ANTHONY ABSOLUTE,	WM. H. CRANE
SIR LUCIUS O'TRIGGER,	NAT. C. GOODWIN
CAPTAIN ABSOLUTE,	ROBERT TABER
DAVID,	FRANCIS WILSON
FALKLAND,	JOSEPH HOLLAND
FAG,	E. M. HOLLAND
MRS. MALAPROP,	MRS. JOHN DREW
LYDIA LANGUISH,	JULIA MARLOWE TABER
LUCY,	FANNY RICE

UNDER THE DIRECTION OF
C. B. JEFFERSON & JOSEPH BROOKS.

January Undermuslin Sale

Carson Pirie Scott & Co.

8

9

10

Visions of a Better Chicago

by Robert I. Goler

The "I Will" sculpture, an emblem of the fair, became a symbol of the pride and optimism that characterized Chicago in the 1890s. Sculpture by J. Fielde, 1892. Facing page: The World's Columbian Exposition recalled the grandeur of Europe and lent elegance to Chicago's lakefront. Photograph by William H. Jackson, 1893.

Chicago in the 1890s was a city of diversity, changing from a city of separate groups and coalitions focused on the neighborhood to a unified populace working to improve the entire city. The process for making this transition was not unique to Chicago, nor was it limited solely to the final decade of the nineteenth century. But as the "Metropolis of the West," Chicago embodied the qualities of growth and expansion that characterized America's conquest and cultivation of the frontier. The city rapidly expanded from a half million souls in 1880 to 1.7 million at the end of the century. This growth paralleled its physical annexation of surrounding communities, prompting citizens to assess needs citywide.

The concern for improving the quality of life in the city reached a watershed in Chicago at the end of the nineteenth century. Through cultural institutions, department stores, new recreational activities, and reform movements, Chicagoans sought to modify and improve their city. The reasons that these visions took hold just a century ago and the forces that made them possible are not completely known, but their manifestations continue to profoundly affect Chicago.

The inspiration for the efforts to improve Chicago lay in the optimistic character of Chicagoans as well as in the city's problems. The same "I

Classical motifs defined the design of the World's Columbian Exposition. These buildings, lining the Reflecting Pool, were modeled on the principles of the Ecole des Beaux-Arts. The sophistication exemplified in the fair announced to the world that Chicago could bring culture to the untamed frontier. Photograph by C. D. Arnold, 1893.

Will" spirit that created the wealth of Chicago and generated the spectacle of the World's Columbian Exposition gave life to new cultural and social experiments. In 1889 the *Chicago Tribune* recognized that citizens now expected "all the benefits of a great city—purer water, cheaper gas, more police and firemen, lower insurance rates, 5-cent car fare, less taxes, more improvements, better drainage, [and] no more typhoid-fever epidemics."[1] The history of the 1890s, in many respects, is framed by the challenges taken up by Chicago's citizens to meet these expectations.

In the final decade of the nineteenth century the city's sphere of influence expanded, and public attitudes about Chicago shifted remarkably.

The growing middle class created the necessary audience for new urban visions and signaled important economic and demographic changes. The new "skyscraper" (a term that first gained popularity in the 1890s) expanded the use of the downtown and influenced the development of department stores. The variety of consumer goods and leisure activities available in the city attracted ever larger numbers of rural and small-town people to the urban environment. The youth of the city adopted bicycling and new styles of dancing and music, breaking away from traditions and revolutionizing the concept of leisure for all age groups and social classes. As the city grew so did the nature of the concerns articulated by Chicago's residents.

The beacon shone brightly at night from the tower of the Electricity Building, demonstrating for all visitors the power of the new technology. Photograph by Gardiner for C. D. Arnold, 1893.

This ivory scepter (c. 1895), with its gold miniature of the fair's Administration Building, was presented to Daniel Burnham to commemorate his coordination of the exposition.

For the first time since the Great Fire of 1871 Chicagoans embraced a progressive civic consciousness. Municipal needs began to supercede individual concerns, a significant shift from the practical, expansionist orientation of Chicago earlier in the century. Private endeavors transformed the city's cultural life, adding new museums, libraries, schools, churches, and an orchestra. But these changes were not sufficient to meet the needs of all Chicagoans.

Beginning with the community-based reforms of the social settlements, new programs quickly emerged from divergent efforts and interests of citizens. An important early example of changing public attitudes was the World's Columbian Exposition of 1893. Inspired in part by the exposition, individuals developed distinct visions of the urban environment. These visions embodied the expectations of the varied groups that composed Chicago, paralleling the range of opportunities that existed in the workplaces and marketplaces of the city. The public need for clean and ethical government prompted citizens to band together in new civic organizations such as the Civic Federation and Municipal Voters' League. The growing interest from different segments of the city's population led to remarkable achievements as people expressed their visions of a better Chicago.

The importance of the 1890s is not that the decade saw each of Chicago's problems resolved but that it spawned a process of change. Individuals and groups who had previously pursued distinct goals now began to focus on similar issues and to build new coalitions. A number of critical social issues, however, were not addressed as citywide concerns during the 1890s. Racial segregation and ethnic discrimination, for example, were ignored by municipal groups until well after the turn of the century. Although many of the goals were not immediately achieved, a new process had emerged to tackle civic problems.

Consensus, however, was not always achieved. Challenges to traditional authority and cultural norms came from many directions and led to a new diversity of voices and viewpoints on matters of public interest. The tensions and issues that resulted from these challenges have contributed to urban life in the twentieth century. Some goals, such as establishing museums and educational facilities for the edification of the general public, have been largely achieved. Other visions, such as the multifaceted consumer culture and the vigorous attention to youth, remain at the forefront of modern American culture. Chicagoans' attempts to begin to shape civic visions at the end of the nineteenth century marked an important shift and helped create the process by which municipal reforms and movements would be defined in the twentieth century.

"The streets will be improved, the great parks of the city will be made still more attractive," proclaimed the conservative *Chicago Tribune*:

Places of popular entertainment will be multiplied. . . . The air will be freed from the smoke contaminations, and the great place of summer resort, with the World's Fair enhanced by all the native charms of the city and the delights of its climate, will be the Paris of America, and such it will remain.[2]

The World's Columbian Exposition combined the city's business values—faith in progress and pride in wealth and in Chicago's growth—and

The Paris of America

The principal planners of the exposition included architects, sculptors, and landscape architects. Left to right: Daniel H. Burnham, George B. Post, M. B. Pickett, Richard Van Brunt, F. D. Millet, Maitland Armstrong, Colonel Edmund Rice, Augustus St. Gaudens, Henry Sargent Codman, George D. Maynard, Charles F. McKim, Ernest R. Graham, and Dion Geraldine.

Burnham's plan for the Chicago fair combined uniform monumental buildings along a strong axis with the greenery of a park.

desire for European cultural forms. To the city's leaders the exposition marked Chicago's coming of age and demonstrated to the world the promise of America's westward expansion. During the latter half of the nineteenth century world's fairs celebrated the major cities of the Western hemisphere. Chicago's ability to secure the world's fair of 1893 marked only the second time a major fair would occur in the New World. Chicagoans welcomed visitors from around the globe to this celebration

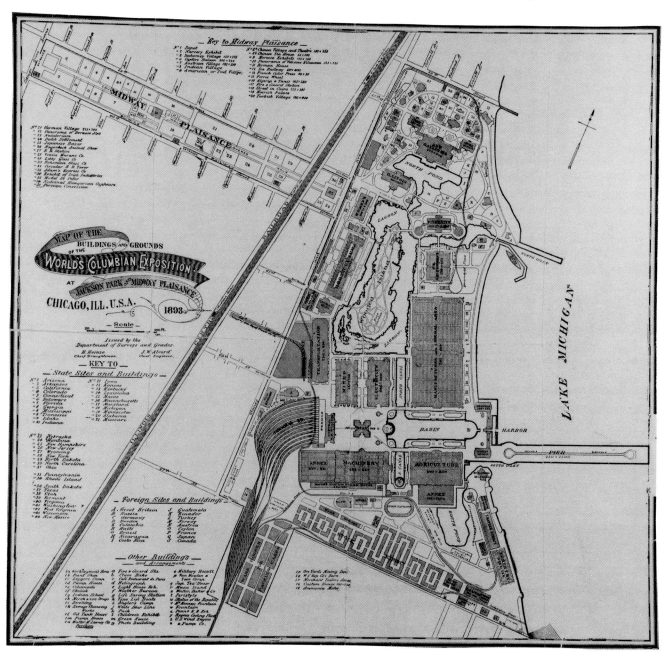

of technological achievements and invited them to evaluate Chicago and its municipal splendors.

As a completely integrated building campaign undertaken by private individuals, estimated to have cost forty-six million dollars, the exposition constituted an important architectural feat in American history and demonstrated the possibilities of urban planning.[3] Situated seven miles south of the Loop, it occupied an enormous tract of land from Fifty-sixth to Sixty-seventh streets, stretching from Cottage Grove Avenue on the west to Lake Michigan on the east. In roughly two years the swampy shoreline had been transformed into an elegant celebration of European aesthetics. Compelling white plaster structures reflected a compendium

The programs below illustrate some of the symposiums sponsored by the World's Fair Congress Auxiliary.

Organized by Reverend John H. Barrows (above), the lectures provided an intellectual aspect to the fair's activities.

of European designs. Modeled on the principles of the Ecole des Beaux-Arts, the fair had been designed by architects, sculptors, and landscape planners, several of whom had studied in France. The undertaking was supervised by Daniel H. Burnham, chief of construction, with important advice from architect John W. Root, landscape designer Frederick Law Olmsted, and engineer Abraham Gottlieb. The collaboration between these different specialists created the unified appearance of the fair.

The central lagoon of the exposition was ringed with numerous buildings created of wood and steel, covered with "staff," a new material that combined plaster, horsehair, and straw, and spray-painted white. Each building maintained a common cornice line, giving a unified appearance to the entire complex. At the center of the lagoon stood a sixty-five-foot statue entitled *Republic*, symbolizing America's rise in civilization.

The exposition proved that planning and money could create order and beauty. It affirmed the assumption of Chicago's leading industrialists and socialites that the problems and troubles of their city could be remedied by private initiatives. This idealism was given concrete expression in a related series of events in the heart of the city. The twenty departments of the World's Fair Congress Auxiliary sponsored over two hundred symposiums on different subjects, from religion to literature, and medicine to economics, that brought the greatest minds of the day from around the globe. "The Exposition will not only furnish an unparalleled spectacle to the eye," remarked organizer Reverend John H. Barrows, "it will also provide for the mind an unequalled feast."[4] These lectures attracted over seven hundred thousand visitors to the newly completed building on Michigan Avenue that had been provided by the Art Institute. The congresses demonstrated the exposition's wish to address issues from an intellectual viewpoint.

Yet the fair did not encompass all Chicagoans; it was a vision created by the business leaders and enjoyed to a lesser degree by other classes of society. The fair's admission price of fifty cents excluded many of the city's workers and the poor, but numerous "nationality days" were proclaimed to attract specific segments of the city's diverse population. This conscious appeal to ethnicity paralleled the strong nationality forums on the Midway and underscored the strong ethnic ties that defined many Chicago neighborhoods. For many Chicagoans the importance of the fair lay in its applications to their lives, through the expansion of the city's department stores, the developing technologies, the innovative forms of popular culture, and the implementation of the new belief in the efficacy of urban planning.

Commerce, Technology, and Progress   The fair's vast display of machines, inventions, and products expressed the belief that progress, through industrialization, could solve human needs. The Liberal and Manufacturing Arts Building, at that time the world's largest building, housed six acres of mass-produced goods. The optimistic perspective on materialism represented by this profusion of products was repeated in building after building on the fairgrounds. Many of the exhibits were for sale, so the exposition was truly an enormous marketplace.

The parallel of the fair to the department store was evident to contemporary observers and to the city's stores. "As the great exposition will leave a lasting impression on the minds of all, likewise shall we make this sale a memorable one," quipped an advertisement for The Fair Store. Downtown stores offered a wide range of materials for examination and purchase in an environment that anticipated the desires of customers and visitors for comfort, convenience, beauty, and order. Some stores associated themselves with the fairgrounds more explicitly; gen-

The Electricity Building, with its bright spotlight, stood on the North Canal near the center of the fairgrounds. Watercolor by Charles Graham, 1893.

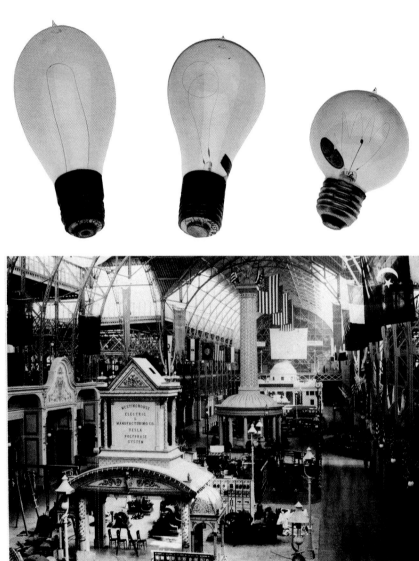

Above: With 120,000 incandescent bulbs, the fair had more light bulbs than the entire city. Right: The interior of the Electricity Building was filled with practical applications of the new technology. Thomas Edison's tower of light (center) demonstrated the brilliance of indoor lighting.

eral information, maps, and rooms for rest were provided for tourists, as were a variety of products exhibited at the exposition.[5]

Nowhere was the exposition's promise of social improvement more apparent than in the Electricity Building. The new technology of electricity epitomized progress, civilization, and a better standard of living. Electricity revolutionized transportation with street railroads, transformed the tools and lighting of the workplace, and improved home lighting.

Electric cable cars first appeared in Chicago in 1890 and had become nearly universally adopted for the city's transportation system by 1892;

by the end of the decade tracks were laid throughout the city, and more than two hundred million fares were collected each year.[6] In 1897 the first electric automobile appeared in Chicago, and electric streetlights were installed on Washington Street. That same year Charles A. Stevens and Brothers began to deliver goods by electric wagons. Not surprisingly, many companies that had turned to electricity to assist their commercial endeavors were principal supporters of the fair.[7]

The fair illustrated the dramatic power of this new technology, as the lighted buildings shone against the dark metropolis. With 6,000 carbon arc and 120,000 incandescent lamps, the fair had more bulbs than the entire city. An ingenious underground system of tunnels accommodated the extensive wiring required for the fairgrounds; electricity was generated within the Electricity Building itself to operate its lamps and machinery.[8]

New electric technology signaled changes in the home and was seen by many for the first time at the fair. Edison's tower of light, an enormous pillar of artificial illumination, was prominently positioned in the middle of the Electricity Building, demonstrating the brilliance of interior lighting. The first all-electric kitchen, exhibited at the fair, foreshadowed the technological transformation of home cooking. The range, skillets, pots, and saucepans all operated through electricity, a significant change toward cleanliness from the wood- or coal-burning stoves of the period.[9]

Another example of electricity's ability to improve modern life and the urban landscape was the movable sidewalk, a covered path that extended almost one-half mile on a pier set in the lake. This invention was intended "to relieve people of the necessity of walking . . . for it is the only really practical device thus far suggested for relieving crowded streets in the congested parts of larger cities." This structure consisted of three platforms that allowed pedestrians to walk on and off without halting the sidewalk's movement: the outermost platform was stationary, the middle one moved at a rate of three miles per hour, and the inner one at six miles per hour, which promoters claimed was "fully as rapid as that of a good cable car, because the latter is perpetually slowing up, stopping and starting again."[10]

The promise of an ever-improving society embodied in technical progress must certainly have found a sympathetic audience in Chicago. Having successfully emerged from the devastation of the Great Fire and flush with the structural achievements of their innovative architecture, Chicagoans were optimistic about their city. The technology of the fair demonstrated new ways to continue the city's advance.

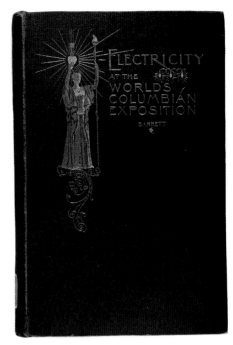

Electricity in the form of a female goddess on the cover of J. P. Barrett's Electricity at the Columbian Exposition *(above). The first all-electric kitchen, containing a stove similar to this early twentieth-century range (below), was exhibited at the fair and promised practical applications for this new technology.*

The movable sidewalk (right) foretold the public improvements that would be accomplished through electricity.

Fantasy, Popular Culture, and the Midway Plaisance   The significance of fantasy must also be considered in relation to electricity at the fair. "The Electrical Building [was] stored with the most marvellous of the marvels of this age," remarked Murat Halsted in *Cosmopolitan*. He continued:

The Fair would be well worthy [of] the attention of the world. Look from a distance at night, upon the broad spaces it fills, and the majestic sweep of the searching lights, and it is as if the earth and sky were transformed by the immeasurable wands of classical magicians; and the superb dome of the structure, that is the central glory of the display, is glowing as if bound with wreaths of stars. It is electricity![11]

The belief that electricity could transform earth and sky inspired great hopes for the technologies powered by electricity and helped to bridge the gap between expectation and reality.

Electricity also changed the way people used their leisure time. Two new forms of entertainment based on electrical power were first seen at the fair: the kinetoscope and the phonograph. These inventions transformed entertainment for the general population by bringing culture to large audiences inexpensively. At the same time, these inventions shifted the control of leisure activities from public to private or individual

The invention of the gramophone by Emile Berliner in 1887 brought music into middle-class homes during the 1890s. [Plate 10]

spheres; the kinetoscope, while generally in a public space, limited viewing to a single participant, and the phonograph brought music into the home. Most important, these technologies allowed people to enjoy themselves on their own schedules.

The kinetoscope, featuring a sequence of photographs seen in quick succession through a viewer, was the precursor of the moving picture shows that evolved over the next decade. Chicago's film magnate, George Spoor, claimed that his interest in making movies was inspired by the kinetoscope at the fair. The ability to record and conveniently replay music on the phonograph quickened the spread of new music and dances. These inventions literally brought cultural forms out of the auditorium and into the home.

From the grand Ferris Wheel to hot-air balloons, the Midway provided entertainment as a contrast to the exposition's educational and technological exhibits.

As an alternative to the order and instruction of the great White City, the adjacent Midway Plaisance provided more pedestrian amusements. A six-hundred-foot-wide strip of land that extended westward from the main fairgrounds to Washington Park, the Midway offered a paradise of ethnology through its extraordinary complex of popular exhibits and entertainments. A series of villages represented many countries, including Austria, China, Egypt, Germany, Holland, Morocco, and Turkey. Exotic extravaganzas made the Midway popular: camel rides and a belly dancer by the name of "Little Egypt" in a streets of Cairo theater, a model of St. Peter's Basilica in Rome, and traditional African music in the Dahomean village.[12]

Midway Ferris Wheel, detail. Built of iron and designed by George Washington Gale Ferris of Galesburg, Illinois, this popular Midway attraction was the first such ride ever constructed. Its central axle measured thirty-two inches in diameter and weighed forty-five tons.

As the centerpiece of the Midway Plaisance, the Ferris Wheel was Chicago's answer to the Eiffel Tower of the 1889 Paris exposition. Built of iron and designed by George Washington Gale Ferris of Galesburg, Illinois, this imposing structure was the first ever constructed; it soared over the Midway, providing unparalleled vistas of the fair and the city. "Up, up, high, higher, highest, and we were two hundred and seventy-five feet in mid-air. Before us were the waters of Lake Michigan," remarked Mrs. Mark Stevens in 1893. "Fronting [us] were the countless

marble-like buildings, and floating from domes and towers were ensigns of every country."[13]

Each of the thirty-six wood-veneered cars measured twenty-seven feet in length, thirteen feet in width, and nine feet in height; together they held a total of 2,160 passengers. The scale of the wheel was appropriately grand for the fair; the central axle alone measured thirty-two inches in diameter and weighed forty-five tons, and the entire structure was illuminated with three thousand bulbs. Two twenty-minute revolutions cost fifty cents, which was as expensive as admission to the main fairgrounds.[14]

A New Vision for the City   The World's Columbian Exposition represented a new vision of urban planning for America, a vision of clarity and rationality. Rarely had artists, architects, landscape planners, engineers, business leaders, and politicians been able to join forces to create a single vision. Its highbrow references to traditional European architecture reflected the aspiration of Chicago's business leaders to give their city a civility that would make it a great metropolis. The great challenge, however, was to put its principles to work in the heart of the city. This challenge began in Chicago in 1893 and continued well into the next century.

The exposition is a potent metaphor for Chicago in the 1890s. As the clean, ordered world of the White City was removed from the congestion and filth of the real city, so the cultured realms of the Art Institute and Chicago Orchestra were havens from the cacophony of the cluttered alleys. The variety of material goods available for purchase prevalent in the exposition's vast exhibition buildings was replicated in the department store with its myriad goods and services neatly arranged to attract customers. As the Midway contrasted with the White City, so too the new dances and leisure activities of the city's youth departed from the cultural pursuits of their parents.

The complexity of the urban vision fostered and required participation of many different groups of society. The organizers of the fair were compelled to complement the White City with the extensive amusements of the Midway, which underscored the important role of general audiences in American culture. The tensions between the cultured metropolis and the gritty city, between the appreciation of beauty and the rush to amusement, and between the hopes of the few and the needs of the many formed a dynamic that recurred in many ways during the 1890s in Chicago.

The Ferris Wheel provided unparalleled views of the fair and the city. Two twenty-minute revolutions cost fifty cents, which was as expensive as admission to the main fairgrounds. Lithograph by The Winters Art Litho. Co., 1893.

Civilizing the City   In the 1890s Chicago's business leaders created and expanded many of the cultural institutions that are so much a part of modern-day Chicago. As products of the final decade of the nineteenth century, each institution was molded by the vision of the founders as well as the needs of the city.[15] For businessmen, "culture" was to be both a sign of their wealth and a civilizer—an antidote to the preoccupation with material gains that had created their wealth.

Chicago had proven its economic might with its wide range of factories, transportation networks, and mercantile services; the city, however, lacked public institutions to spotlight its cultural achievements. Many of the city's leaders had traveled abroad and had cultivated an appreciation for the traditions of Europe. The Armours, Fields, Hutchinsons, McCormicks, Palmers, and Ryersons were among those who collected paintings and decorative arts to bring antiquity and cultured tastes to their homes on the shores of Lake Michigan.[16] The city's businessmen and their wives wanted cultural amenities to enhance their lives and to trumpet their own success.

In response to this perceived need to provide the amenities of a great city, leading citizens established or expanded a substantial group of institutions in the 1890s. These included educational organizations such as the Armour Institute, Kent School of Law, and The University of Chicago, as well as sites such as the Garfield and Lincoln Park conservatories. Two particularly significant aspects of culture in this decade—arts

From left to right: Martin Ryerson, Cyrus Hall McCormick, Philip Armour, Marshall Field.

and social sciences—were brought about by private initiatives and would have moral, enlightening influence on the general community. Although both women and men saw the significance of developing arts and education in the city, the major participants in cultural philanthropy were men. The man controlled most of the family's money, even if the bulk of it was his wife's family inheritance. The social involvement of women was limited to ameliorating the suffering of children and the elderly.[17]

Borrowing models from cities of the East Coast and Europe, these men sought to make Chicago's civic institutions among the finest in the world. The institutions were housed in structures reflecting the European travels of the city's elite; the forms were neoclassical, neo-Gothic, or Romanesque, not Chicago's indigenous steel-frame skyscraper. The grandeur of these buildings emphasized the unrivaled ability of the wealthy to work on a monumental scale. Physically, these institutions emulated the ideals of the World's Columbian Exposition; the fair's architecture had embodied a vision of order and culture, as seen in Baron Georges-Eugene Haussmann's rebuilt Paris. The new structure of the Art Institute, built with funds provided by the exposition and the Art Institute's trustees, hosted the symposiums of the World's Fair Congress Auxiliary. After the fair, the Field Columbian Museum occupied the Fine Arts Palace in Jackson Park.

Central to the vision of the city's leaders was the assumption that the arts were morally uplifting. They fervently believed that the institutions

they created would be beacons for the less fortunate in Chicago. This translated into concerted efforts to make the new cultural amenities accessible to all Chicagoans. Reaching new audiences was necessary to successfully implement the civilizing mission of these organizations, and these institutions opened their doors to all of the city's residents. The reduction of the average work week from sixty to fifty-four hours during the latter half of the nineteenth century and the decreasing cost of material goods through industrialization gave more people more time and money for leisure and culture.[18] The central location of many of these new cultural institutions on trolley and elevated lines provided easy access from most parts of the city. Underlying these efforts was also a hope that cultural amenities, such as the newly established Chicago Public Library, would assist in the self-improvement of Chicago's citizens. In time the middle- and working-classes came to represent important segments of the audiences and funding of these institutions.

Facing page above: The Art Institute building (1893), with its neoclassical facade, echoed the European ideals that some Chicagoans strove to adopt for their city. Left: Students at the School of the Art Institute (c. 1895) were encouraged to draw live models, a progressive position in nineteenth-century America.

European Arts in the Midwest   The Art Institute was the business elite's vision of a European museum, a nineteenth-century invention that would serve as a palace of culture. First established as the Chicago Academy of Design, this organization was restructured and renamed the Art Institute of Chicago in 1882. After the World's Columbian Exposition the Art Institute moved into the building at Michigan Avenue and Adams Street. Designed by the Boston architectural firm of Shepley, Rutan, and Coolidge, the new building systematically massed the galleries around a central courtyard and stairwell, creating an effect of grandeur and logic. The relocation of the Art Institute into its new structure was a watershed in the institution's history because it gave physical expression to the efforts of the trustees to create beauty in their community.[19]

Under the direction of Charles L. Hutchinson, work began to assemble a permanent collection of art. During the 1890s the purchase of the Demidoff collection, the early acquisition of an El Greco canvas, and life-size plaster casts of prominent sculptures were exhibited in the galleries to further this European aesthetic. Significant loan exhibitions from the community's private collections augmented these artworks. Among these were paintings of the Barbizon school and the Impressionists, which dramatically challenged the traditional depictions of pictorial reality. These contemporary works reflected the travels and tastes of the

Established by leading Chicagoans to bring morally uplifting art to the city, the Art Institute was led in its early years by Charles Hutchinson (facing page below). Within the galleries (below, c. 1900), all Chicagoans could view the art of Europe.

EXHIBITION OF BLACK&WHITE
DRAWINGS BY   SCHMEDTGEN
             HOLME✗✗✗
             McCUTCHEON

AT THE ART INSTITUTE
JAN 26 TO FEB 21
ILLUSTRATED ✗
CATALOGUE✗✗✗

Above: Exhibition poster, c. 1897. In addition to its collections of European works, the Art Institute frequently included local artists, such as newspaper illustrators, in its exhibitions.

city's leaders and formed the strong nucleus necessary for a permanent collection.

With an ambitious schedule of exhibitions and public programs, the Art Institute reached a broad audience and quickly established a strong membership. After the exposition the Illinois General Assembly mandated free admissions for schoolchildren and one free day admission for the general public each week. By the end of the decade 2,300 Chicagoans had pledged their annual support, and by 1910 annual attendance surpassed that of the Museum of Fine Arts in Boston and the Metropolitan Museum of Art in New York.[20]

Illustrated stereopticon lectures, gallery tours, and craft demonstrations were offered to the public four or five days each week. Local artists, including newspaper illustrators William Schmedtgen, Frank Holme, and John T. McCutcheon, were also represented in the Art Institute, and an early selection from the Chicago Arts and Crafts Society, founded at Hull-House, was exhibited in 1897.

In addition to the permanent collections of the Art Institute, the institution also established an art school. Students worked from the art in the galleries as well as from live models, the latter a progressive practice for late nineteenth-century America. Through its permanent collection and art school, the Art Institute attained a special role in the city's cultural life as both promoter and preserver of the fine arts.

Serious Music for Chicagoans   Inspired by the World's Columbian Exposition and the spotlight that it would shine on Chicago, the city's leaders rushed to establish a symphony orchestra that would bring European musical taste to the city. Since mid-century Chicagoans had enjoyed classical music, but no musical organization had been able to attain financial security. As a companion to fine arts, music was an essential element of a cosmopolitan city, and businessman Charles Norman Fay successfully garnered the backing of the city's wealthy residents for this endeavor. He promptly attracted Theodore Thomas, a German-born virtuoso who had established a solid reputation as a violinist and conductor in New York, and who had, for the past two decades, brought an orchestra on tour to Chicago. Thomas created a proficient orchestra in Chicago, bringing many of his instrumentalists from New York.

Thomas's goal of educating the people of Chicago to his vision of morally uplifting music resulted in his insistence on performing complete orchestral pieces, primarily German, especially the music of Brahms, Beethoven, and Wagner. Despite the city's large German population, residents had become accustomed to the light and episodic concerts of French and Italian composers, and these new programs drew occasional complaints. "One ought not to mind the criticisms of these stupid persons," scolded the conductor's wife. "Mr. Thomas is here to establish a great *Art work*, & to make Chicago one of the first musical centers of the world—and *not* to provide a series of cheap musical entertainments for the riff-raff of the public. The highest forms of art . . . are not within the comprehension of the masses. . . . All that can be done is to *produce it*, & let it stand till the ignorant acquire a little education & begin to understand it."[21]

But Thomas recognized his responsibility to expose the unaccustomed to the moral qualities of classical music. To expand the audience for the orchestra he inaugurated a series of "Workingman's" or "People's Concerts"; all of the Auditorium's four thousand seats were filled at the reduced admission of ten to twenty-five cents when the first of these was held in 1893. Only the price was cut; the programs were undiluted.[22]

The large size of Dankmar Adler and Louis Sullivan's Auditorium, however, ultimately proved a disadvantage to the orchestra. It was rarely

The Chicago Orchestra, led by Theodore Thomas (above), performed on the main stage of the Auditorium Theatre through the 1890s (below). Photograph by Lawrence and Dinius, c. 1899.

Right: The Auditorium Building (c. 1895). Designed by Louis Sullivan and Dankmar Adler as a multipurpose building, the Auditorium included offices, a hotel, and a major performance hall.

Right: Man's top hat and gloves, opera glasses, and 1894 orchestra programs. Chicago's wealthy businessmen created cultural institutions to serve as an antidote to the preoccupation with material gains and to provide gathering places (below). The Graphic, March 17, 1894.

possible to fill the seats, so people did not feel the need to purchase advance subscriptions; this situation restricted the orchestra's cash reserves, which limited Thomas's ability to make firm plans. At the turn of the century construction began on the smaller Orchestra Hall to enable the orchestra to operate with greater efficiency. The new building was designed by Daniel Burnham and opened on December 14, 1904. Thomas, however, did not live to fully enjoy the new hall, for just three weeks after opening night he died of pneumonia.[23]

The New Social Sciences   Chicago's leaders valued the new social sciences of the late nineteenth century, such as economics, anthropology, and sociology, and designed two institutions to pursue the new academic disciplines: the Field Columbian Museum and The University of Chicago. In some respects the practical, scientific qualities of these disciplines paralleled the brash directness that had characterized Chicago's growth. The decision to focus attention on new disciplines, therefore, represented the ability of the city's leaders to look forward. The

Established after the World's Columbian Exposition, the Field Columbian Museum occupied the fair's Fine Arts Palace (c. 1895).

social sciences emerged as important fields at the end of the nineteenth century; Chicago's new institutions attracted distinguished professionals to the Midwest.[24] From this strong beginning Chicagoans soon developed a reputation in those fields that would last into the twentieth century.

Using the cultural collections of the 1893 exposition as its core, a natural history museum was established in 1894 in the fair's Fine Arts Palace in Jackson Park. The museum remained in that structure until moving to its current site in Grant Park in 1920. With the donation of one million dollars from Marshall Field, the institution adopted its benefactor's name and was able to take over the Fine Arts Palace, which had been more substantially constructed than the other exposition buildings

Ayer Hall (c. 1895) in the Field Columbian Museum featured important collections of North American Indian material. Anthropologists viewed the Indians as a disappearing people whose way of life should be documented.

because it had housed great works of art. A collection of plaster casts from the World's Columbian Exposition depicting events of Columbus's life were placed on view in the central rotunda to focus attention on the explorer. Other installations on technical and social progress complemented the natural history holdings. The Industrial Arts collection focused on technological achievements of the Steam Age. Large engines, such as those of trains, demonstrated the technical progress of America and Europe over the preindustrial cultures on view in the anthropological wing. The collections of specimens demonstrated the development of biological evolution, while the underlying ideology expressed was Social Darwinism. The message of the fair and the museum were similar: America (and Chicago) was at the apogee of the cultural hierarchy of human history.

Research was a major endeavor of the museum, especially in the fields of anthropology and archaeology. The staff presented their findings through exhibitions that were organized by geographical location. The museum amassed large collections of ethnographic materials from cultural groups around the world. Objects were displayed in exhibition cases with aluminum labels to clearly identify the objects and to make them accessible to a wide audience.

The anthropological work of the Field Columbian Museum embodied a new appreciation of American Indians as a group of "disappearing peoples" whose ways of life should be documented.[25] This perception, at the forefront of contemporary anthropology, contrasted sharply with the antagonistic stance of Chicago a generation earlier, when memories of the Fort Dearborn Massacre were still vivid. By the end of the century, however, Indians were no longer a historic foe but an anthropological subject. This change in philosophy underscored the new belief that the American frontier no longer existed, a point eloquently made by Frederick Jackson Turner at his famous 1893 address on this subject delivered before the American Historical Association in Chicago.[26]

In The University of Chicago the business leaders sought to create an institution that would bring educational excellence to their city. Land was donated by Marshall Field (originally valued at $150,000), and an endowment gift of $600,000 was received from John D. Rockefeller, Sr. The city's prosperous merchants and industrialists joined forces to make this vision of cultural advancement a reality. In addition to Field and Rockefeller, the principal contributors were William Ogden, Martin Ryerson, and Charles Hull; important support also came from Charles Yerkes, Sidney Kent, and Charles Hutchinson.[27] Built adjacent to the

Frederick Skiff, the Field Columbian Museum's first director, headed a staff of researchers in the new social sciences. The findings of their research were made accessible to a wide audience in the museum's galleries.

Right: William Rainey Harper, shown here in 1901 accompanying John D. Rockefeller, Sr., across the University of Chicago campus, diligently cultivated the support of wealthy donors and succeeded in attracting distinguished scholars to Chicago. Below: Although it boasted of its accessibility to the Loop by streetcar, the university was designed to be a haven from metropolitan commerce and congestion. Drawing by Henry Ives Cobb, 1893.

Midway on the city's South Side, the university represented a haven from metropolitan commerce and congestion.

By the time of the Columbian Exposition the physical plan of the university could easily be discerned. A major influence on its development was the appointment of Henry Ives Cobb as architect for the university. Cobb constructed new buildings for a variety of prominent cultural institutions during the 1890s, including the Chicago Historical Society and the Newberry Library, and drew upon Gothic and Romanesque traditions of architecture. For the university he developed an English scheme, recalling Oxford and Cambridge by adopting a uniform style of neo-Gothic architecture.

While Cambridge and Oxford were its architectural models, the new university emphasized the new social sciences and built a strong reputation in the field. President William Rainey Harper, a professor of Greek recruited from Yale University, attracted a distinguished group of scholars in these new disciplines, including Thorstein Veblen and John Dewey. The preeminence of The University of Chicago's social science program brought substantial credit to the founders in the early twentieth century as the city lent its name to a branch of the new discipline that became known as the Chicago school of sociology.

Under Harper's direction the university's curriculum encouraged traditional classical studies along with innovative approaches to the social and physical sciences. A major library collection was assembled as were

Henry Ives Cobb (above) designed buildings for many cultural institutions in the city. For the University of Chicago he applied the models and medieval traditions of Oxford and Cambridge universities, endowing the campus with a uniform architectural style. Above left: Hutchinson Hall, Mitchell Tower, Reynolds Club, and Mandel Assembly Hall. Photograph by Barnes-Crosby, c. 1905.

Regalia, such as the detail from this University of Chicago ceremonial mace, underscored Chicago's desire for European traditions.

research laboratories. The first courses were offered the autumn semester of 1892. Through its commitment to social science research, the university recognized the similarities of the city's different educational groups and forged ties with the surrounding community. Harper sought to extend this relationship to Chicago's new and diverse cultural institutions by establishing a forum at the university of the principal administrators and trustees from the Art Institute, Field Columbian Museum, and Chicago Orchestra.[28]

The university also expanded ties to the community through its extension program, by which faculty members spoke to groups across the Midwest, and the Laboratory School, established by John Dewey to implement his new hands-on educational approach. This process continued after the turn of the century when Graham Taylor, founder of the Chicago Commons social settlement, was invited to lecture beginning in 1903.[29]

With the Art Institute, Chicago Orchestra, Field Columbian Museum, and The University of Chicago, the city's leaders had created significant cultural institutions for improving the quality of life for the general public and for elevating Chicago's reputation. These institutions raised the general awareness of and appreciation for culture and education. Yet they did not speak to issues that affected the lives of all Chicagoans. Other coalitions soon formed to address these conditions.

Below: Hull Court at the University of Chicago. Photograph by Barnes-Crosby, 1905.

"Shop windows are full of a thousand wonders for a boy of ten," remarked one commentator in 1905. "If he can never own the toys in the flesh he can possess them in spirit as he flattens his nose against the plate glass."[30] The lure of the Loop, with its burgeoning shopping palaces, saloons, dime museums, and general exuberance, was irresistible. The diverse opportunities for material possessions were a leveling component of late nineteenth-century urban life; anyone could participate in the marketplace if they had the money or the desire. Opulence was there to see and touch, if not to buy. Even those who did not participate could hardly ignore the profusion of goods. Young boys peered into plate glass windows, women browsed in department store aisles, and couples mingled at the city's many theaters. The excitement of commerce and entertainment in the downtown attracted immigrants, transients, residents, and visitors alike; each came with expectations that could be fulfilled in the metropolis: the promise of materialism.

The architecture of the Loop expanded remarkably in the 1890s. The increased building height, made possible by the innovation of structural steel at the end of the 1880s, led to a greater density of buildings and people along the streets. Increased numbers of workers held jobs in the central business district, a situation that helped spawn the growth of downtown department stores. Ease of transportation to and from the city's center was critical to the success of stores and theaters. Most were

The Promise of Materialism

Marshall Field's department store provided the finest luxury goods, such as this silk evening gown (above, c. 1899), to Chicago's wealthy citizens. The addition of large plate glass windows attracted pedestrians and made it possible for people of all classes to be lured by material goods (left). Photograph by Barnes-Crosby, c. 1905.

located within the compact confines of the Loop and could be reached by railroad or streetcar from virtually any part of the city.

Downtown also attracted tourists, as well as the many who traveled through Chicago to another destination, for by 1893 Chicago had come to represent the new metropolis as much through the vigor and energy of its bustling business district as through the White City. "Those who go to study the world's progress," an observer remarked in *Harper's Weekly*, "will not find in the Columbian Exposition, among all its marvels, any other result of human force so wonderful, extravagant, or peculiar as Chicago itself."[31]

The Thrill of the Marketplace   A major attraction of Chicago was the panoply of shopping emporiums and the wide range of material goods available. Chicago provided access to jobs, and jobs provided Chicagoans with the money to buy the items available in the private market.

In the marketplace of the Loop individuals felt a sense of participation. The ability of the individual to choose from a variety of goods, to purchase items with cash or credit, or even just to window-shop helped expand public participation and expectations. The introduction of large street-level display windows at several department stores attracted pedestrians and invigorated the urban landscape, making it possible for anyone to be drawn to the lure of material goods.

Elegant display cases helped to promote the latest fashions in Marshall Field's, c. 1900 (right). The department store became known for stocking a wide variety of merchandise of the highest quality, and it attracted not only Chicagoans, but also tourists. Above, women's hats, typical of those sold at Marshall Field's, c. 1890.

With the opening of Marshall Field's State Street department store, every individual who entered the store could now see, touch, and—if they had money enough—take home the finest goods money could buy. Field's store not only served the wealthy with the finest of European imports, but it displayed this genteel elegance for the less well-to-do, raising the material expectations of the lower and middle classes. Retail sales of quality materials remained limited well into the twentieth cen-

Acquiring goods became a focus of working- and middle-class life, and department stores sought to expand their audience, using methods such as this sale poster from Carson, Pirie, Scott and Co., c. 1900 (left). Above: Clothes typical of those worn by middle-class women, c. 1890. [Plate 8]

The Big Store covered an entire city block and housed merchandise on nine floors (right, 1893). Above and facing page, right: The popularity of sporting goods grew as people enjoyed greater time for leisure activities at the end of the century.

tury, but Field's more than made up for this with an enormous wholesale business. And as one of Chicago's major tourist attractions, Field's began in 1895 to display luxury even to the passerby in its striking window displays.[32]

A variety of extensive retail department stores catered to the middle class. Among these was The Big Store, operated by Siegel, Cooper & Company; this establishment covered the entire city block on State Street from Congress to Van Buren. Merchandise was organized on nine levels and was carefully arranged to anticipate the needs of customers, much as it is in a modern shopping mall. This compact and efficient

In the new department stores of the Loop, customers could choose from a variety of goods, purchase items with cash or credit, or just window-shop. Lithograph by W. L. Carqueville, c. 1900.

shopping emporium encouraged customers to see individual goods within the context of the complete home environment. Linens and toiletries, intended specifically for women of leisure, were conveniently located on the first floor for quick impulse purchases. Hats, corsets, and other ladies' goods were upstairs, followed by an extensive array on the third floor that included sports equipment, art supplies, luggage, and even a doctor's office. Furniture was available on the fourth floor and, in an attempt to promote one-stop shopping, foods ranging from fresh fish to cereals to fruits provided convenience on the fifth floor. The uppermost floors were used primarily for storage and business operations. The lower level contained household goods such as hardware and crockery. Customers could eat at the cafe on the lower level.

Acquiring goods became a focus of working-class life, and the department stores sought to expand their audience. Several department stores and mail-order houses issued small printed pieces, such as calendars and pocketbooks, to thank patrons and to encourage future purchases. Their message of consumerism foreshadowed the large-scale advertising of the twentieth century.

The mansions of Chicago's wealthy residents became show places of the riches the industrial order could create. Interior of the Marshall Field mansion.

Owning a Home: Real Estate and Subdivisions In the half-century following the Civil War, Chicago's population increased twentyfold and the city limits spread out from the lakeshore through the process of annexation. The influx of immigrants meant that Chicago had more Bohemians, Croatians, Danes, Dutch, Germans, Greeks, Lithuanians, Norwegians, Poles, Slovakians, and Swedes than any other American city, and its population of African-Americans was growing at double the rate of whites.[33]

To meet the resulting demand for housing, new structures rose in neighborhoods on all sides of the city. While not all people maintained their ethnic identities, strong neighborhood cohesion developed and remains a characteristic of modern Chicago. Poles settled to the northwest, Czechs and Italians to the southwest, European and Russian Jews to the west, Germans to the near north, Scandinavians further to the north and west, and African-Americans to the south. The newest arrivals would often move into ramshackle cottages, tenements, or overcrowded apartments. If circumstances permitted, they could move to more pleasant neighborhoods with two- and three-flats and the occasional detached single-family structure.[34]

For many people owning and furnishing a home represented the fulfillment of their urban expectations. Nationwide, slightly more than one

For many people owning and furnishing a home represented the fulfillment of their dreams for urban life. Many middle-class citizens imitated the fashions of the wealthy in their single-family homes or row houses.

of every three families owned their own home during the 1890s.[35] By the 1890s the enormous pressure for commodious housing exploded in a development boom that enabled Chicago's real estate market to meet every taste and level of expenditure. At one extreme the city was a show place of the new wealth that the industrial order could create, from the mansions of the Glessners and Pullmans on Prairie Avenue to the sumptuous windows of Marshall Field's department store. Chicago's wealthi-

Samuel Eberly Gross, Chicago's master builder of the late nineteenth century, proudly marketed his developments to specific audiences. In this advertisement from 1883, he appealed to German residents and immigrants.

est citizens lived in a world of closed carriages, private schools, exclusive clubs, reserved church pews, opera boxes, and grand houses. For them consumption was conspicuous, with mock castles and chateaux on Prairie Avenue. By the end of the decade more of the new mansions were built on the new North Side "Gold Coast," following the lead of Potter Palmer, whose massive Romanesque castle proudly faced the lakefront.

The middle class often imitated the fashions of the wealthy in their single-family homes or row houses. In the final decade of the nineteenth century the enormous physical expansion of the city and the concurrent arrival of immigrants led to significant new real estate developments. Samuel Eberly Gross, Chicago's master builder of the late nineteenth century, developed numerous "subdivisions" for both the middle and working classes. He designed a variety of floor plans for families of different sizes, incomes, and social pretensions. The walls of his office at Dearborn and Randolph streets in the Loop exhibited a range of house designs emulating the order and spaciousness that characterized the residences of the wealthy.

By the early 1890s Gross could boast of having sold more than thirty thousand lots and built ten thousand houses. These homes ranged from simple workers' cottages to moderate homes with neocolonial facades, and each had the essential elements of a respectable home: an entrance

Easy access to the Loop by streetcar was an important element of urban subdivision developments (right, 1899). Among the many homes offered to Chicagoans were a working-class cottage in Avondale (left, 1891) and a middle-class house in Gross Park (center, 1891).

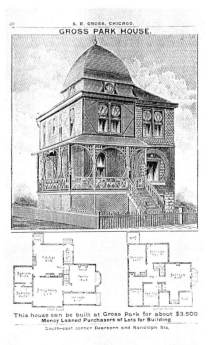

The middle and working classes could furnish homes with copies of the latest fashions, such as this kerosene lamp, c. 1890, and parlor suite, 1891. Furniture was made more affordable by Chicago's massive furniture industry.

vestibule, sitting room or parlor, kitchen, pantry, and bedrooms. These homes could be bought for as little as one hundred dollars down and ten dollars a month. Many took advantage of the inexpensive balloon-frame construction by which houses since midcentury had quickly risen on a frame of prefabricated lumber assembled with mass-produced nails.[36]

The middle and working classes could furnish homes with copies of the latest fashions, turned out by Chicago's massive furniture industry. Furniture, lamps, drapery, kitchenware, and all the objects essential to a genteel domesticity could be purchased in Chicago's department stores as well as in less elegant neighborhood shops. To accommodate such purchasers stores often provided financing that permitted payments to be made over a period of time. By making it easier for people to purchase, local businessmen met individual needs while expanding the market for their goods.

For many Chicagoans, however, the hope of owning their own house remained just a dream. Throughout the city rental units in two- and three-flat buildings sheltered most of the city's working-class families. Others lived in tenements, boarding houses, and rooming houses with

Swedish immigrant Matts Thorsson and his family are shown in their home at 664 North Wells, 1898.

few worldly goods. Those who could not afford new furnishings obtained second-hand merchandise at street stalls, such as those on Maxwell Street. Such Chicagoans owned only a few changes of clothes, and these were used by the household in one form or another until ready for the rag man.

The promise of the city, then, was closely tied to the vitality of the urban economy. As long as the economy was strong, a wide range of options remained available to people of different levels of society, and the vision of upward social mobility was evident from the self-made men of the city and the diversity of merchandise offered in stores.

The Lure of the Loop   Nightlife was important to the residents of Chicago in the 1890s, and the focus of that activity was downtown. Though nighttime in the city had long been considered dangerous, the introduction of electric lighting brought a sense of security to the city's streets and ameliorated citizens' fear of darkness.[37] The completion of the electrification of the elevated railways within the Loop in 1897 further increased accessibility to its attractions.

The clear and bright illumination provided by electricity also increased the social acceptability of nightlife in the city. Several traditional urban entertainments, such as frequenting saloons and brothels, were not acceptable for women. But among the popular amusements of the 1890s, several were appropriate for men and women to enjoy together. Theaters, dance and music halls, and dime museums each had their allure, and the improved lighting encouraged women to go out at night.

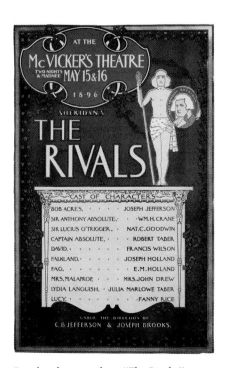

Popular shows, such as "The Rivals," (above, 1896) attracted both men and women to one of the few amusements acceptable for women in the 1890s. [Plate 7]

Theaters, such as the Arcade at 156–64 Clark Street (1892), provided a rare opportunity for members of different economic classes to mingle; the sumptuous decor surrounded everyone with the image of wealth.

Theater was especially significant because the range of ticket prices brought members of Chicago's different classes together under one roof. The theaters were clustered in the Loop, and shows were offered weeknights at 8:15 P.M.; Saturday matinees began at 2:00 P.M. General admission to most shows was 75¢, with reserved seats available for up to $1.50, and more exclusive boxes for $10.00 to $12.00. The productions of numerous theater companies, augmented by such luminaries as Sarah Bernhardt and Lillian Russell, supported a number of Chicago theaters throughout the decade. The occasional side show, such as that of strongman Eugen Sandow ("the perfection of physical manhood"), also attracted popular attention.

"The freaks of all climes are to be found on exhibition," noted one writer describing Chicago's numerous dime museums, "and most of the museums throw in a stage performance of some kind more or less meritorious."[38] Dime museums, with collections of curiosities, were intended for a diverse audience. They had existed in Chicago since the 1840s, predating the institution of the art museum, and continued to be popular at the end of the century. The Eden Musée featured extensive wax works that were said to rival those of London's Madame Tussaud. During the 1890s this collection was combined with a stage show and restaurant and operated as The Casino. An important example of these museums was the Libby Prison War Museum, established by Charles Gunther in 1889. Gunther had amassed a significant collection of Civil War memorabilia, and he moved a Confederate prison from Richmond, Virginia, to exhibit his holdings.[39]

Chicago could boast of three large panoramas during the 1890s. These enormous murals were installed in circular rooms and occasionally were supplemented with reconstructions at their bases to enhance their realism. One of the more popular of these was a depiction of the Battle of Gettysburg. In an age that relied heavily on static images, and in which the moving image was only just emerging, such visual illusions had wide appeal.[40]

Among the less refined entertainments were burlesque, minstrelsy, and vaudeville. Although intended for male audiences, these forms of entertainment dated from the mid-nineteenth century, and by the end

In Chicago of the 1890s, the Loop provided a variety of entertainments. Weight lifters such as Eugen Sandow (above) entertained theater audiences. Trocadero Theater program, 1893. Below: This souvenir card from the Eden Musée, a dime museum, recalls a horror exhibit.

To house his extensive Civil War collection, Charles Gunther moved the Confederate Libby Prison from Richmond, Virginia, to Chicago. The Libby Prison Museum became one of Chicago's most popular museums of this period. Illustration from The Graphic, *May 28, 1892.*

of the century it had become acceptable for both sexes to attend such shows.[41] Burlesque involved seductive performances of female sexuality as well as caricatures of well-known figures. Dressed in provocative and revealing clothes, these women mingled song and dance with an occasional striptease in their steamy presentations. Minstrelsy consisted of men in blackface caricaturing the activities of blacks, often through the antics of the fictional personalities of Tambo and Bones.

Vaudeville transformed into a family show in the 1890s as a modified version of the bawdy variety shows of the saloons. Designed for family audiences, shows consisted of dancing, singing, magic and animal performances, and humor; as with minstrelsy, the humor was often ethnic and racist.[42]

As the heart of the city, the Loop was the central focus of material achievement during the 1890s. From the ordered hierarchies of the department stores to the interlocking structure of the elevated trains and transit system to the new subdivisions and expanding city, the central business district offered many things to many people. Alternatively, to those with limited incomes—the immigrants, laborers, and unskilled workers, who rarely could afford the time or expense of visiting downtown—the possibility of possessing newer and finer goods remained tantalizingly out of reach.

As the nineteenth century was ending, young people of many backgrounds patronized new amusements that distinguished them from the predominantly ethnic world of their parents. The new amusements that they chose were the first steps in the creation of a mass culture that would virtually replace the separate cultures of ethnic groups and social classes in the twentieth century.

These new forms of entertainment that emerged in the 1890s enabled both middle- and working-class individuals to participate. The proliferation of products and information in the late nineteenth-century urban environment, the anonymity of work, and the repetition of activity in the industrial workplace contributed to the creation of what has been called "mass popular culture."[43] Mass production methods made many of these amusements available at a reasonable price, and the regimen of the factory environment prompted many younger members of society to seek new emotional and physical outlets.

This change was possible because money and leisure were now available to Chicago's youth. Middle-class youths received spending money from their parents while many working-class youths had their own jobs. Successful efforts to reduce the workday to ten hours, as well as only a half-day on Saturday, gave people more time to enjoy cultural pursuits and leisure.[44]

The first manifestations of this new culture were the bicycle craze, dance halls with new music, and amusement parks. These developments highlighted the shift in values that elevated leisure over work, widened the sphere of unmarried, young women's activities, and increased a couple's opportunities for time alone. Young women could enjoy freedoms denied to their mothers: athletics, dancing, and drinking in public. The resulting shifts in courtship characterize the modern era.[45]

The Bicycle Craze   The bicycle craze of the 1890s was not just a hobby of a few individuals, but a public phenomenon. The development of the safety bicycle in the late 1880s with two equal-sized wheels and pneumatic tires meant most healthy individuals could ride it, unlike earlier high-wheel models that required unusual physical coordination. The structure of the safety bicycle also allowed women to ride unassisted. This offered new freedoms of athleticism and movement to more women and opened the doors to new sexual mores. With little opportunity for privacy between courting couples in the nineteenth century, the bicycle was especially appealing to young people.[46] It offered opportunities to meet members of the opposite sex unchaperoned, helping to reshape

The New Culture of Youth

Bicycling offered a new way for men and women to meet unchaperoned. The El Dorado Cycle Co. published this sheet music by John Quinn and Adam Craig, c. 1896.

The structure of the new safety bicycle (top right) made it possible for women to ride unassisted, providing new freedom of mobility. Couples had little privacy in Victorian America; the side-by-side bicycle (bottom right), c. 1890, provided couples with an opportunity to be alone. Below: Bicycle bloomers (1887) gave a new freedom to women's clothes at the turn of the century.

courtship patterns. Advertisements frequently portrayed young women cyclists and described the freedoms of loose-fitting bloomers and of self-propulsion, which compounded the bicycle's allure.[47]

Catering to the burgeoning group of riders, a variety of companies manufactured bicycles in Chicago in the 1890s, including Crescent Bicycles, Monarch Cycle Company, and Western Wheel Works. Although the cost of forty to seventy-five dollars put new models out of reach for most of the working class, bicycles became immensely popular among the middle class, and second-hand models found their way to working-class neighborhoods. By the end of the decade, Arnold, Schwinn & Company reported production rates of one million bicycles each year. Indeed, the efficiency of the safety bicycle even led the city to establish a bicycle corps of policemen.

Bicycling group, c. 1893. These groups became a popular way to enjoy this new sport and meet new people. Chicago had no less than five hundred cyclist clubs by 1895.

Above: *Advertisements for bicycles frequently portrayed young women cyclists and described the freedom of self-propulsion, a novelty in the 1890s and a major factor in the bicycle's allure. [Plate 6] Lithograph by Will Denslow, 1895. Right: Illustration from a bicycle catalog, c. 1895.*

The enormous popularity of the bicycle established new forums for communication within the community. The *Inter-Ocean* began a regular newspaper column on bicycle races in 1897, and many of the bicycle clubs in the city issued magazines. *Wheel Talk*, for example, was founded in 1895 "to inject into the cold atmosphere of business life the warmth of personal kindliness"; this publication reached ten thousand enthusiasts and included articles on bicycle-related products as well as "practical points" from its readers.[48]

The proliferation of bicycles fostered the creation of bicycle clubs, supply stores, and agitation for more bicycle paths in public parks.[49] As a national center for the manufacture of bicycles, Chicago had no less than five hundred cyclist clubs by 1895. Enthusiasts could join organizations such as The Hermes Club or the Chicago Cycling Club, the oldest such organization in the country, for fifty cents a month (after the five dollar initiation fee). Catering to the need for maintenance and repairs, a string of stores opened on Madison Street offering accessories such as a spare tire ($6.50), a brass kerosene lamp ($2.25), a tire repair kit (5¢), or a bell (25¢).[50]

Dance Halls   From the more respectable cakewalk competitions to the dance halls of neighborhood saloons, young people listened to new music and danced new steps in the 1890s. A number of new dances gained popularity in the late nineteenth century: the rumba, the tango, the one-step (or turkey trot), the two-step, the fox trot, the quick step, and the cakewalk. These dances were faster than their predecessors, with rhythmic motions that deviated from the smooth glides and turns of the waltz and led the way to the ever-popular ragtime of the turn of the century. These vigorous, dynamic innovations in music and dance were outlets to the strict discipline of factory, office, and family life.

More than other new amusements, dance and music, with their suggestions of sensuality and ties to liquor, challenged the morality of Vic-

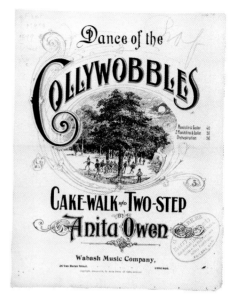

Rooted in African-American traditions, the cakewalk mimicked Southern courtship rituals. Although perceived as threatening to established society, it became immensely popular in the 1890s. Above: Sheet music by Anita Owen, 1899. Below: Illustration from Frank Leslie's Illustrated Newspaper, 1899.

Popular literature exposed the dangers of the new dances that became popular among the youth of the 1890s. The dances challenged the morality of Victorian America and the cultural values of the parental generation. From the Ball Room to Hell *by T. A. Faulkner, 1894. Below: Dance dress, c. 1895.*

torian America and the cultural values of the parental generation. Moralists were quick to criticize them. One diatribe against dancing, *From the Ball Room to Hell*, underscored the pernicious lasciviousness that was believed to tempt the youth of Chicago.[51] "It is a startling fact, but a fact nonetheless, that two-thirds of the girls who are ruined fall through the influence of dancing," remarked T. A. Faulkner, a veteran dance master. Faulkner warned parents not to allow their children to learn the new dances, for the "beautiful girl who attended the dancing school as pure and innocent as an angel three months ago, returns to her home [one] night robbed of her most precious jewel of womanhood—virtue!" Having fallen so precipitously, "she has no longer any claim to purity; her self-respect is lost; she sinks lower and lower; society shuns her, and she is today a brothel inmate, the toy and plaything of the libertine and drunkard."[52]

No dance was more threatening than the cakewalk. This dance evolved from creole traditions in New Orleans at the end of the nineteenth century. The dance was rooted in African-American traditions, but promoters sought to create interest in a sanitized version for northern audiences. One advocate described a suitable cakewalk as "not one or two poorly-clad couples giving a fierce exhibition, or a short-skirted concert hall soubrette giving a vulgar imitation of high kicking, but a refined rendition of Southern courtship in the long ago."[53] Chicago's youth were quick to adopt this dance, and it soon gained incredible popularity with citywide competitions during the 1890s.

Amusement Parks   Inspired by the Ferris Wheel and the Midway at the World's Columbian Exposition, amusement parks developed rapidly in Chicago. Immediately after the fair a series of small, single-theme parks were scattered throughout the city. The economic depression of the 1890s, however, limited their continued success.

The exposition had established beyond doubt the public's enjoyment of mechanical entertainment and fantasy settings, and, with the upswing of the economy at the turn of the century, a new group of larger, elegant parks emerged. The substantial capital investment that they demanded reveals the size of the new leisure market. Some parks, such as the prominent White City, which opened in 1905, explicitly imitated the fair through classical design. Its attractions included two dance floors and a roller-skating rink, as well as The Chutes, a ride in which men and women climbed a tower, descended a steep water slide in small boats, and passed beneath a European-style bridge before coming to rest in a

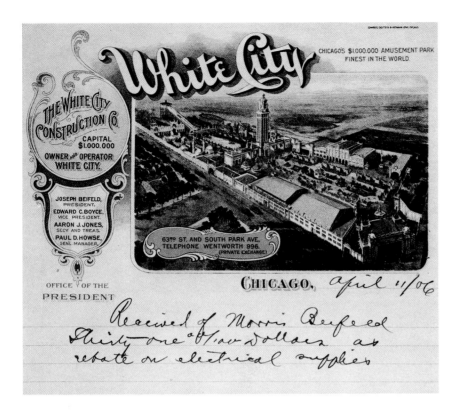

The White City Construction Company used this depiction of its famous amusement park, which imitated the World's Columbian Exposition in its classical design and its name, on their letterhead in the early twentieth century (left). Below: The Chutes at the White City Amusement Park. Men and women climbed a tower and descended a steep water slide in small boats, splashing into the basin below. Photograph by Barnes-Crosby, c. 1905.

Essanay Studio badge, c. 1910. Inspired to experiment with making moving pictures by Thomas Edison's kinetoscope, George K. Spoor founded Essanay Studios in Chicago in 1897. For a brief time Chicago reigned as the nation's film capital.

large basin. Soon other chutes appeared in the city, such as the one at Jackson Boulevard and Kedzie Avenue, where each ride cost ten cents.

Perhaps the most extravagant of these leisure parks was Riverview Park, founded in 1903 on a seventy-two-acre site at Western and Belmont avenues. The diversity of its rides and diversions attracted large crowds. The greatest crowd pleaser was The Scenic Railway, an early roller coaster. Amusement parks met the popular demand for thrills by literally throwing men and women against each other; the rides mastered the mechanical technology of the day and, through their exotic facades and imagery, placed participants within a world of fantasy.[54]

This interface of technology and amusement culminated with the invention of moving pictures, a form that provided darkened privacy for young couples at an affordable price. Chicago was one of the early centers of motion picture production as well as audience interest. The early films were black and white, silent, and generally ran only a few minutes in length. Vaudeville audiences saw these films, interspersed between minstrel and burlesque acts.

Building on the work of the Lumière brothers in France, William Selig created the world's first movie studio in Rogers Park on Chicago's North Side in 1897. His first film was a short called *Tramp and Dog*. The studio rapidly expanded, and by 1907 Selig had moved to larger facilities at Irving Park Road and Western Avenue, where he operated the largest studio in the country.

That same year Essanay Studio was established in the city, making Chicago the nation's film capital. Essanay's founder, George K. Spoor, had first become interested in motion pictures at the Columbian Exposition, where he had seen Edison's kinetoscope. Billy Anderson, Max Linder, Tom Mix, Gloria Swanson, and, for a short period, Charlie Chaplin worked in the Essanay and Selig studios. California's year-round mild weather and the development of new independent studios contributed to the decline of Chicago's film industry by the outbreak of World War I, but not before it had indelibly altered the character of modern American popular culture.[55]

The New Civic Consciousness

In the 1890s a new civic consciousness that encompassed many different strata of society emerged. Citizens, recognizing their public responsibility, established several coalitions to effect change in the city. A critical element of these coalitions was that they drew from a variety of segments within the community. Limited efforts began to transform municipal government into an agent for effective change. This shift from private to public responses was evident in several activities and gained momentum as distinct groups of individuals acted on behalf of their concerns. The most significant of these efforts sought to improve living conditions throughout the city, respond to the needs of urban children, and eliminate corruption in municipal government. Though these conflicts did not galvanize all levels of society or replace the system of ward politics, they forged a new dimension of public accountability that evolved into the Progressive movement after the turn of the century.

Urban Laboratories   In the late nineteenth century a new breed of social reformers sought to overcome the social divisions and conflicts of the city. Women and men, shocked by the poverty and harshness of Chicago life, worked to make Chicago more humane. They pioneered a new institution in the 1890s: the social settlement.

The thirteen-building Hull-House complex, c. 1905. Jane Addams and Ellen Gates Starr founded the first settlement house, a new institution created to provide services to poor neighborhoods in the nineteenth century. Photograph by Barnes-Crosby.

Following the example set by Jane Addams and Hull-House, Mary McDowell (right) founded the University of Chicago Settlement to serve the immigrant poor. Many social reformers came from middle-class backgrounds; all believed that residence among the poor was essential to understanding their needs. Below: The Hull-House Coffee House, c. 1900.

Jane Addams and Ellen Gates Starr founded the first settlement house in Chicago, Hull-House, on Halsted Street in 1889. They were soon joined by others, including Florence Kelley, Julia Lathrop, and Alice Hamilton, who sought to build bridges between the middle class and the working class, between the native-born and the immigrants. In the 1890s Graham Taylor founded Chicago Commons, and Mary McDowell started the University of Chicago Settlement. Gads Hill and the Northwestern University settlements soon followed. All operated on a similar premise; residence by the educated and socially conscious among the poor would instill the knowledge needed to provide necessary services.

The settlements became the source of both a critique of the quality of life in Chicago and solutions to particular problems. Many of the social reformers, like William Stead, had a religious basis for their criticisms, but all shared a sense that what was lacking in Chicago was the direct, face-to-face community that existed in small towns. They believed that when people lived together, they learned to understand and sympathize with one another, and to work together. Seeing that the class-segregated neighborhoods of the industrial metropolis made such knowledge impossible, the reformers lived at the settlement houses they created in the midst of the slums.[56]

The settlement houses all sought a scientific basis for their activities. The reformers pioneered social survey research to understand the problems of their neighbors and to have a firm basis for action. The first major studies, done at Hull-House in the 1890s, produced information on wages and working conditions in the area, which led to Florence Kelley's fight for regulation of the garment industry. She became Illinois's first factory inspector and was instrumental in curbing child labor and the epidemics of disease spread by sweatshop conditions.

Although the social reformers were sympathetic to the problems of labor, their concerns were broader than the workplace. The program of the settlements was as varied as the imaginations of its young staff as they sought to deal with all the needs and desires of their neighbors. Hull-House, for example, was a veritable "department store of humanitarianism."[57] Its 1895 program included college extension courses, a reading room branch of the Chicago Public Library, art exhibitions, a "working people's chorus," concerts, piano lessons, cooperative boarding houses for working women and men, lecture series, groups to influence labor legislation and encourage unionization, ward improvement clubs, social clubs for adults, children's clubs, a savings bank, cooking and sewing classes, a free kindergarten and day nursery, a playground and summer excursions for children, a gymnasium, a public dispensary, and a labor museum.[58] This program spoke to the impoverished life of slum dwellers. They needed efforts to enhance not only their work lives, but also their family lives and their leisure pursuits.

Through their programs the social settlements spearheaded civic reform in Chicago during the 1890s. Beginning with community-based programs that responded to the immediate needs of the local residents, they demonstrated that practical improvements could be made. Among these were quality-of-life issues such as savings banks and playgrounds, as well as public health concerns of pure milk, disease prevention, and sanitation. Several of these became rallying concerns for many different neighborhoods and segments of the population, and in time they were the models for subsequent municipal programs.

Public Health and "The Eighth Wonder of the World"   To address the public health concerns that were recognized as a major urban problem at the end of the century, groups such as Hull-House educated immigrants about disease prevention. Private measures such as these, however, were limited in their effectiveness because they did not correct the environmental problems that caused the diseases. The need for new approaches to solving urban problems was evident.

The dramatic impact of waterborne diseases crossed social and economic barriers and, with the growing understanding of Robert Koch's theory of germs, led to the formation of coalitions to improve sanitary conditions and reduce infant mortality in Chicago. Clean water was seen as the single factor that would improve the health of the greatest number of Chicagoans. As a result public support for the Sanitary Canal was overwhelming.

The Sanitary District was formed in 1889 to plan the project, and ground was broken for the canal on September 3, 1892. This massive construction project of a twenty-eight-mile canal from Chicago to Joliet was designed to divert the Chicago River—with its raw sewage—to the Des Plaines River, thereby preserving the purity of the city's drinking water from Lake Michigan. Approximately sixty thousand cubic yards of dirt and stone were removed each day to a depth of 30 to 35 feet and a width of 160 to 202 feet. The canal was twice the width of the Suez Canal and required the removal of more soil and rock than would the Panama Canal. The total cost for the project was estimated at twenty-nine million dollars, making it "the greatest [engineering project] undertaken by a single municipality."[59]

Rampant waterborne disease prompted Chicagoans to support the building of the Sanitary Canal, a massive undertaking for any city at the time. This ceremonial shovel was used to remove the first and last piles of dirt from the canal in 1892 and 1900.

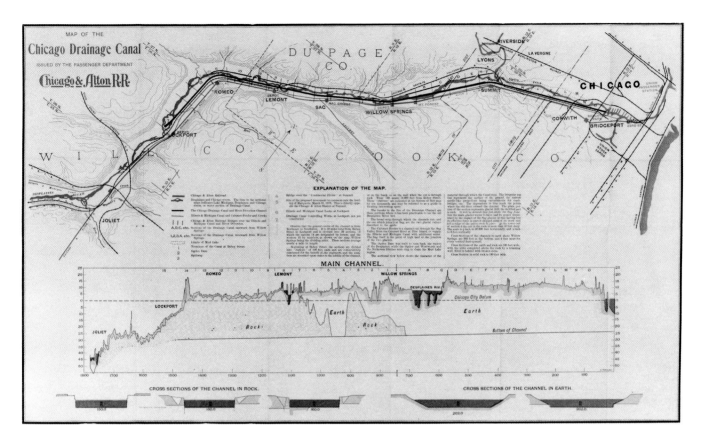

The canal ran twenty-eight miles from Chicago to Joliet, diverting the Chicago River to the Des Plaines River (above, 1895). Left, construction crews removed sixty thousand cubic yards of dirt and stone each day. Below: Gold badge presented to commissioner William Boldenweck during the 1890s.

The project was completed on January 1, 1900, and its success was noted by engineer B. A. Eckhart as "in every way meeting our most sanguine expectations. The water in the Chicago River . . . is as blue as the sky above us."[60] Though crude by modern standards, the canal effec-

As an antidote to the environment of the slums, Hull-House opened the city's first playground in 1894 (top). Supervised recreation was an essential element in early playgrounds. Play equipment and climbing apparatus from the first playground, at Polk Street near Halsted Street, provided an opportunity for physical exercise (bottom, c. 1895).

tively dispersed the city's sewage in sufficiently large quantities of water to dramatically reduce the incidence of waterborne diseases in Chicago and death rates during the summer.

Helping the City's Children   Spurred by the rapid industrialization and population growth of the late nineteenth century, Chicago's slums worsened and the city's alleys grew more foul. After visiting Chicago, reformer William Stead wrote, "The first impression which a stranger receives on arriving in Chicago is that of the dirt, the danger, and the inconvenience of the streets."[61] Social settlements spearheaded the attempts to improve living conditions in the city.

The size of the city and the isolation of tenement neighborhoods effectively closed off Chicago's poor from major parks and beaches. A study published in 1898 determined the disproportionate distribution of parks in the city. While 95 percent of the parks were within one mile of the lakeshore where only one-third of Chicagoans lived, two-thirds of the city's residents shared approximately 5 percent of the urban parks, representing a density of 4,720 individuals to each park acre, a figure greater than the most congested part of Calcutta.[62]

Relatively few elderly people lived in Chicago in the 1890s, and 40 percent of the population was under twenty years of age. In the neighborhoods served by the settlements, neglected, overworked, and delinquent youths were common, and the settlement houses soon focused on the problems of youth.

Settlement houses initiated the establishment of playgrounds to provide structured, sanitary alternatives to the filth of the alleys. In addition to reasons of health benefits, it was believed that access to parks would instill qualities of morality and citizenship in the city's youth. "A boy robbed of his chance to play will not be an honest and effective citizen," remarked reformer and photographer Jacob Riis before the Merchants Club in 1899. "You can't depend on him at the polls."[63]

Hull-House opened the city's first playground in 1894 on land donated by William Kent. A second playground was opened two years later by the Northwestern University Settlement, followed by a third in 1898 organized by the University of Chicago. Much like the city's many German Turner gymnasiums, these playgrounds often included climbing apparatus, play equipment, handball courts, indoor baseball, and asphalt surfaces. Adult supervision was a critical component of this approach for it was important that children's activities be structured, just as their environments; Hull-House, for example, arranged for residents or local

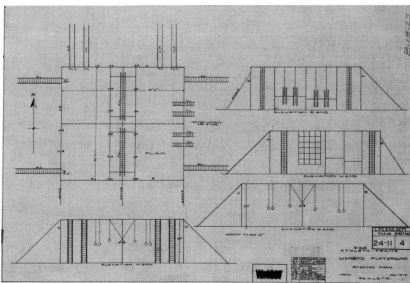

Providing places for children to play became a public concern in the 1890s. Eventually the city followed the Hull-House example and built play equipment for its parks. These plans (left) were drawn for the gymnastic equipment in Stanton Park, 1911. Playground at Morgan Street and Grand Avenue (above) was operated by Chicago Commons, c. 1901.

Louise deKoven Bowen (above), a wealthy society lady, emerged as a leading advocate for reforming the legal system in Chicago to protect juveniles. Photograph by Max Platz.

police to oversee the activity of children in the playgrounds.[64]

The settlements also exposed urban children to the pleasures of nature, with the expectation that such an experience would provide proper moral underpinnings. Gads Hill, for example, sponsored a summer camp in Elgin for 265 boys and girls. For $4.50 (two-thirds of which was paid for by the settlement) a child could spend two weeks in the fresh air. Chicago Commons sponsored outings to escape "the breathless congestion of sun-baked city centers." For those who could not afford to leave town, they arranged for "friends in country towns . . . [to] send baskets and boxes of flowers to be distributed where they will do the most good."[65]

Another reform that successfully raised the status and protection of children was the creation of the juvenile court system. This new judicial system identified delinquent youths and granted them options more appropriate to their age than they would receive in the adult courts. A principal protagonist of this reform was Julia Lathrop of Hull-House. The Juvenile Court was first established in Cook County in 1899 in a courthouse directly across the street from Hull-House. The detention center had a gymnasium and a school; probation officers, provided by Hull-House, monitored the young offenders.

The creation of the juvenile court system was the culmination of a generation of increasing concern for the welfare of Chicago's children. Louise deKoven Bowen, a wealthy society lady, emerged as a leading advocate for juvenile reform in Chicago and lobbied hard at City Hall and in Springfield for legal measures to protect children. The achievement of the court system through the political and legal channels of the state demonstrated the growing sophistication of reformers.[66] This approach was soon adopted by other cities around the country.

Creating Concerned Citizens   In the 1890s coalitions of Chicagoans attempted to educate and involve citizens in the reform and maintenance of clean, ethical government. These groups generally worked independently of each other, but they sought a similar response from a wide populace.

Foremost among those groups that promoted clean government was the Civic Federation, established by business leaders in response to William Stead's public lectures on vice and immorality in Chicago. "Every effort should be made from the start," noted a contemporary advocate, to avoid "the impression that [the] 'Civic Federation' is a piece of scholastic idealism. It must be a business man's plan and the other elements should keep in the background."[67] The underlying assumption, however, that the federation would provide a single standard that would appeal to all audiences suggested a moral code that was not actually in place throughout society. Although an important first attempt at building civic unity, the coalition of reformers and business leaders subsequently fell apart.

The Municipal Voters' League, founded in 1896, took direct stands on partisan issues.[68] The League focused directly on the positions of public officials and published accounts of politicians' voting records to enable citizens "to decide which of these members of the Council should be retired from further public service." In explaining the League's charges of "boodleism" (a contemporary term for corruption) against Thirteenth Ward alderman E. W. Stanwood, the League's president, George Cole, summarized the goals of the organization:

Our standard, [that] only aggressively honest and capable men [should be considered] for city officials may now by comparison seem high, but we believe it to be the only true one. We may not at once secure such candidates in all cases, but we can at least make public the records of all candidates.[69]

The League identified twenty-six of the thirty-four aldermen running for office in 1899 as corrupt. Through a dedicated campaign of education, sixteen of the incumbents were defeated. The League proceeded to challenge the remaining ten aldermen and, in the subsequent election, retired four more. The success of this approach led journalist Lincoln Steffens to remark that Chicago was "half free and fighting on."[70]

The movement for responsible government culminated in the public debates over awarding public franchises for metropolitan services. The most significant of these controversies to surface in the 1890s concerned control of the city's streetcars. The introduction of electricity led to the development of "grip" cars that moved by means of an underground cable system. The streetcar routes were operated by private companies under franchises from the city. By the 1890s the most prominent operator was Charles Tyson Yerkes, who had assembled traction companies in the city and expanded his influence by constructing 250 miles of track under the charters of eight different companies. He later merged these holdings into the Chicago Consolidated Traction Company, creating one of the largest streetcar systems in the country.[71]

The issue of franchise awards revolved around concerns about crowded and unsafe conditions on the cars and the threat of fare in-

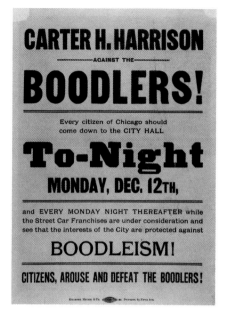

In the 1890s Chicagoans worked to rid the government of its corrupt officials, or "boodlers." Attempts at reform brought Chicagoans together against a common problem.

George Cole (above), president of the Municipal Voters' League, led the crusade against corruption in city government.

creases. Public outcries against Yerkes reached enormous proportions when he requested that the city grant him an exclusive franchise for fifty years. Such a franchise would be substantially longer than the usual twenty years and would ensure Yerkes and his associates millions of dollars in profit. When the issue came before the city council in December 1898, the public thronged the balcony and hung nooses over the side to impress their intentions upon the aldermen. Yerkes' proposal was defeated, and the prospects for more lucrative franchise awards were slim; Yerkes sold his holdings for fifteen million dollars the following year and moved to New York.[72]

The mobilization of the public for responsible government had proven itself in this confrontation and demonstrated to the city's aldermen their need to protect public interest. During the first two decades of the new century, citizen groups such as the Civic Federation and Municipal Voters' League sought greater changes by amending the city charter to be more responsive to public expectations.[73]

Planning a Better Metropolis   During the nineteenth century groups of private individuals had formed to establish public parks. Municipal leaders developed Lincoln Park in the 1860s and, in 1869, created three park commissions to preserve a ring of parks surrounding the city. Throughout this period, however, such civic efforts remained isolated, and the parks remained beyond the reach of the working-class residents of the "river wards."

The movement for responsible government culminated in the traction fight of the late 1890s. Charles Tyson Yerkes (above, c. 1895) sought complete control of the city's streetcar routes by bribing city officials. When the issue came before the council, the public filled the balconies of the council chamber (right) to impress their opinions on the aldermen. Photograph by George Lawrence, 1898.

Beginning with Hull-House's initiatives, providing adequate space for the children of immigrants to play and grow became a public concern in the 1890s. Building on Hull-House's activities, municipal school properties were opened after school for neighborhood children in 1897.[74] Only in 1899 did the city's three park commissions agree to join forces to create new parks in tenement neighborhoods. Complementing the growing interest in the playground movement, many of the new parks included gymnastic equipment, field houses, running tracks, baseball diamonds, and swimming pools. The three commissions subsequently merged in the twentieth century to form the Chicago Park District.[75]

The appreciation for public parks and recreation prompted expanded initiatives within the city. This shift from private initiatives to public

Lincoln Park, c. 1890. The appreciation for public parks and recreation and the desire to improve the city ultimately led to a shift from private efforts to create recreational facilities to a broader support for such government programs.

These design proposals for Michigan Avenue, painted by Jules Guerin for the 1909 Chicago plan, illustrate the uniform architecture and wide boulevards that Burnham envisioned for the city. [Plate 9]

consensus of civic improvement paralleled the emergence of modern urban planning. Flush with the success of the World's Columbian Exposition, Daniel Burnham and his young associate Charles Atwood began to plan for a major reshaping of Chicago's physical organization.

Beginning in 1896 Burnham presented pieces of this plan, the first comprehensive urban vision for the Chicago lakefront and related municipal functions, to the city's leaders. While these proposals did not immediately capture the imaginations of the business leaders, their principal elements were revised in Burnham's famous 1909 plan for the city. Its subsequent success incorporated the ideals of the City Beautiful movement, a loosely allied group of designers who felt that rational and

attractive civic planning would elevate feelings of citizenship. In a very real sense Burnham's great plan of 1909 can be interpreted as the physical and spiritual culmination of efforts by the leaders of the 1890s to establish in Chicago the high culture and milieu of a great city.

By the dawn of the twentieth century the concern for public policy and amenities had undergone a significant change in Chicago. From the visions of private individuals, embodied in the cultural institutions that flourished in the 1890s, came the more comprehensive visions of the World's Columbian Exposition, for which planning occurred on a citywide basis. The yearnings for citywide improvements soon found expression in clean government, the Sanitary Canal, and playgrounds.

Conclusion

The attempts to make Chicago work for all of the municipality's residents cut across traditional divisions within the community. Ethnic leaders joined forces with business leaders to celebrate nationalities at the exposition. Social reformers combined their energies with those of the manufacturers to insure the safety and reliability of streetcar service. But these were only beginning gestures.

The seeds of the modern era were sown in Chicago during the final two decades of the nineteenth century. The creation of the youth culture in the 1890s meant new directions and assimilation for second-generation immigrants. The excitement of the department stores of the Loop reflected a new attraction to material goods and consumption and made more pitiful the plight of the poor.

Many important municipal needs, however, were not resolved during the 1890s. Among these were racial segregation, poor working conditions, and urban planning; these would not be directly confronted until well into the twentieth century. The importance of the 1890s, however, lies in the development of new forms of citywide dialogue. Groups and individuals from different backgrounds, neighborhoods, and ethnicities found themselves face-to-face with other representatives as they met at the social settlements and worked together at the Municipal Voters' League. While much remained to accomplish, the optimism of the decade and the visions of the city's many groups raised the level of civic pride as Chicago entered the twentieth century.

Afterword

by Ellsworth H. Brown

Is Chicago of the 1990s, like Chicago of the 1890s, at a crucial juncture?

In the 1890s Chicago was a city in transition; the need for change was great. Lacking civic unity, Chicago nonetheless had two elements—leaders and optimism—that enabled it to accomplish change. In the last decade of the nineteenth century, it developed from a city of a million strangers to one that managed to work together to institute the most basic of city services. In addition, private groups pursued improvements. It does not matter that this change, from a cluster of communities to a city unified in its essentials, was not complete; it was remarkably successful in terms of the nineteenth century. The combination of realized needs and civic like-mindedness created the most powerful decade in this city's history.

The purpose behind this exhibition and catalogue—the first in a biennial series that will lead our visitors and readers out of this century and into the next—is not only to explore the past through its objects and ideas, but also to consider how the past can inform the future. To accomplish this goal and the new mission thus suggested, we have paired the Society's forces with the most able scholars.

Therefore we are compelled to ask the questions anew. No doubt, we are today the metropolis of the Midwest. But what of our civic unity, our sense of community? Does our city demonstrate care for the welfare of the public as a whole?

And if the answers to these questions are not all that they could be, we must ask whether Chicago, one hundred years later, is still a city that can successfully gather strangers together to address public needs.

To assert that 1990 is a turning point because of the century's impending passing is insufficient and whimsical, but to assert that 1990 is a time of crisis on its own terms is valid. The basic human problems of the 1890s remain on the books today, often in more extreme forms. Consider the catalogue of difficulties.

The two decades share profound differences between rich and poor. The class differences of the 1890s came out of a new manufacturing society that was unregulated and stretched the limits of old systems. Today's differences exist despite limits, systems, and attitudes that argue against the widening gap of personal fortunes that, we are told, increases continually.

Racism remains a deep and disturbing problem. In the nineteenth century, a tiny minority of the population was other than white. If racism was less obvious it was only because of its less frequent occurrence, for it was unfettered and undisguised. Notwithstanding the force of law, growing public understanding, a more open political process, and a more active press, Chicago today remains a divided city. In a report issued in 1989, the Chicago Community Trust said Chicago is "one of the most racially segregated metropolitan areas in the United States."[1]

Ethnic tensions remain, too, intermingling matters of race into a complex and therefore difficult subject. In 1890 most immigrants to this city of a million strangers came from eastern Europe. They bore their share of abuse, but strength in numbers and the assimilation of second or third generations into the mass of native Chicagoans eventually ameliorated their condition. In the 1990s this container, still not a melting pot, holds a new mix of immigrants who must cope with questions not only of ethnicity,

but also of race to a degree unknown a hundred years before.

Education was a problem and remains so, but for different reasons. One hundred years ago it was the tool by which society transmitted American cultural values and tried to combat juvenile delinquency and child labor. Today we look to the schools not only to transmit societal values, but also to provide the knowledge necessary for success in a world of complex machines and processes. Despite recent attempts at educational reform, without doubt Chicago's schools are in trouble. A crucial juncture could not be more clearly defined: the *Chicago Tribune* reported that Secretary of Education William Bennett called Chicago's schools the worst in the nation.[2]

Health and sanitation, the living conditions of individuals, child care, the dilemmas of one-parent families, epidemics, and crime in its several forms—the full range of human concerns have remained active for the last century. Given the perpetual state of these urban issues, one might ask whether the 1890s were as successful as the exhibition and this catalogue represent them to be. The answer is yes.

In the 1890s Chicago came to a turning point and *changed*, setting precedents and establishing solutions never before considered in

public terms. Faced with the need to think about problems as common responsibilities, city leaders invented new tools. In the 1890s Chicagoans were without service or regulatory government agencies (or the attendant tax structures). They had a handful of laws to combat child labor and no laws or practices to deal successfully with workers' strident demands. Likewise, immature Chicago also lacked cultural amenities. Finally, Chicago did not yet have many of the community and private organizations that would make such a difference in the lives of countless individuals. By the end of the decade, significant progress had been made on all fronts.

In contrast, the Chicago of 1990 has many tools. Cultural agencies abound, the product of those who hoped they would be forces for good in a needy city. Tax structures have changed radically, and with the changes have come a network of city, county, state, and federal agencies charged with helping those in need, with regulating, correcting, and enforcing. The press is more inquisitive and aggressive, less inclined to validate the established order. Private agencies exist, from Hull-House (created in the 1890s) to a vast if never sufficient array of other nonprofit and church organizations.

If simple analogies sufficed, the

prospects of the 1990s would be high. But in his introduction Sam Bass Warner suggested that one crucial thing has not remained constant: the nature and locus of authority. In the nineteenth century authority was vested in a few men who, through force of personality, position, and wealth, dominated business and government. They were owners, not managers. They had the right as well as the means to make decisions of any kind. They enjoyed a unique ability to effect change, to determine the course of events and the solutions to problems, to develop the systems and controls. As Sam Bass Warner said, they "believed that in the city of Chicago one could gather like-minded strangers together, and that together they could make their city a richer and better place."

To effect change, the leaders needed only to become aware of the challenges and the merits of meeting them. Because their society was tight and readily identified, leaders of reform could reach the leaders of the city in a relatively straightforward way. With persistence, the Reverend Stead advanced his cause through preaching, and Jane Addams found access through the Civic Federation. If the leaders of industry and government composed a small, closed, and sometimes un-

fair society, they were nonetheless efficient and optimistic and, to a large degree, accountable only to themselves.

If the nature and locus of authority in the 1890s was enabling, its current state makes more difficult the application of the many tools available in 1990. Modern society places great emphasis upon pluralistic values, emphasizing the merit of many different visions. The resulting dispersal of authority, wider participation in government, and heightened demands and expectations of disparate groups—often to the exclusion of each other—treats many visions equally at the expense of forces on behalf of a few, focused public goals. This is especially true in government, which responds most immediately and completely to public pressures.

The rapidity and thoroughness of governmental metamorphosis has widened the gap between the corporate model, less required to change, and government. Nonetheless, business leaders have not been immune to the forces of change. Obliged in varying degrees to public expectations and legal requirements, these leaders are less able to act independently than their predecessors of the last century. Managers, often more able than their predecessors, are often unable to act with the conviction of owners. The individual's

vision, which brought so much power to the 1890s, can be diminished by a host of things: taxed, and thus lower, profits; stockholders' activism and rights; greater media scrutiny; more complex laws and regulations; a mature union structure; and a more competitive and complex business environment. Thus in business, as in government, the possibility of achieving a few overriding and commonly shared goals is diminished in 1990.

The diversification of authority has made it possible for neighborhood and citizen organizations to become an additional force in society, sometimes for good and progress and broad civic causes, and sometimes for smaller, narrower, or retrogressive ideas. Either way, they are now part of the web of authority that we must confront to achieve solutions to problems.

All of this is not to suggest that the answers of the 1990s ought to be the answers achieved in the 1890s. This is not possible. But if history means anything, and if the Chicago Historical Society's exhibitions and catalogues are to do more than chronicle things past, we should consider the perspectives and attitudes of those nineteenth-century friends who helped shape our Chicago, as we contemplate this century's closing decade.

Notes

Foreword

1. Wayne Andrews, *Battle for Chicago* (New York: Harcourt, Brace and Co., 1946).

The Metropolis of the West

1. Ray Ginger, *Altgeld's America: The Lincoln Ideal versus Changing Realities* (New York: Markus Wiener Publishing, Inc., 1986), 248–53.
2. William Thomas Stead, *If Christ Came to Chicago* (Chicago: Laird & Lee, 1894), 466.
3. Carl D. Buck, *A Sketch of the Linguistic Conditions of Chicago* (Chicago: The University of Chicago Press, 1903), 14.
4. Humbert S. Nelli, *The Italians in Chicago, 1880–1930* (New York: Oxford University Press, 1970), chap. 1.
5. Edward R. Kantowicz, "Polish Chicago: Survival through Solidarity," in *Ethnic Chicago*, ed. Melvin Holli and Peter d'A. Jones, rev. ed. (Grand Rapids, MI: William B. Eerdmans Publishing Co., 1984), 214–38.
6. Christiane Harzig, "Chicago's German North Side, 1880–1900: The Structure of a Gilded Age Ethnic Neighborhood," in *German Workers in Industrial Chicago, 1850–1910: A Comparative Perspective*, ed. Hartmut Keil and John B. Jentz (DeKalb: Northern Illinois University Press, 1983), 127–44.
7. Sam B. Warner, Jr., *The Private City* (Philadelphia: University of Pennsylvania Press, 1968), chap. 6.
8. Odd S. Lovoll, *A Century of Urban Life: The Norwegians in Chicago before 1930* (Northfield, MN: Norwegian-American Historical Association, 1988), 54–73.
9. Ellen Skerrett, "The Catholic Dimension," in *The Irish in Chicago*, ed. Lawrence J. McCaffrey et al. (Urbana: University of Illinois Press, 1987), 22–60.
10. The Archdiocese of Chicago, *A History of the Parishes of the Archdiocese of Chicago* (Chicago: Catholic Bishop of Chicago, 1980), passim.
11. Irving Cutler, "The Jews of Chicago: From Shtetl to Suburb," in Holli and Jones, 69–108.
12. Edward Mazur, "Jewish Chicago: From Diversity to Community," in Holli and Jones, 46–68; Cutler, "Jews of Chicago," 69–108; Ira Berkow, *Maxwell Street: Survival in a Bazaar* (Garden City, NY: Doubleday & Co., Inc., 1977), 1–84.
13. Kantowicz, "Polish Chicago," 214–38; Joseph J. Parot, "The American Faith and the Persistence of Chicago Polonia, 1870–1920" (Ph.D. diss., Northern Illinois University, 1971), chaps. 1–3.
14. Joseph Wandel, *The German Dimension of American History* (Chicago: Nelson-Hall, 1979), 90–94.
15. Harzig, "Chicago's German North Side," 141; Perry R. Duis, *The Saloon: Public Drinking in Chicago and Boston, 1880–1920* (Urbana: University of Illinois Press, 1983), 154–55.
16. Chicago Board of Education, *Annual Report for 1892–93* (Chicago: 1893), 123–62.
17. Michael F. Funchion, "The Political and Nationalist Dimension," in McCaffrey et al., 61–97.
18. Bruce Nelson, *Beyond the Martyrs: A Social History of Chicago's Anarchists, 1870–1900* (New Brunswick, NJ: Rutgers University Press, 1988), chap. 4.
19. Nelli, *Italians in Chicago*, chap. 6.
20. Michael F. Funchion, "Irish Chicago: Church, Homeland, Politics, and Class—The Shaping of an Ethnic Group, 1870–1900," in Holli and Jones, 14–45.
21. Ulf Beijbom, *Swedes in Chicago: A Demographic and Social Study of the 1846–1880 Immigration* (Stockholm, Sweden: Laromedelsforlagen, 1971), 266–87.
22. Lovoll, *Century of Urban Life*, 105–38; Beijbom, *Swedes in Chicago*, 266–87.
23. Buck, *Linguistic Conditions*, 4.
24. John Higham, *Strangers in the Land* (New York: Atheneum, 1965), chap. 4.
25. Broadside, *Swift for Mayor* (Chicago: Headquarters of Loyal American Legion, 1895) Chicago Historical Society Prints and Photographs Collection.
26. Skerrett, "Catholic Dimension," 22–60.

27. Letter from Paul Morton to J. Sterling Morton, Nov. 22, 1893, Morton Family Collection, box 13, folder 3, Chicago Historical Society Archives and Manuscripts Dept.

28. *Lakeside Annual Directory of the City of Chicago* (Chicago: 1896), 48.

29. Allan Spear, *Black Chicago: The Making of a Negro Ghetto, 1890–1920* (Chicago: The University of Chicago Press, 1967), part 1.

30. Ida B. Wells, *The Reason Why the Colored American is not in the World's Columbian Exposition* (Chicago: Ida B. Wells, 1893).

31. Duis, *The Saloon*, 157.

32. Ida B. Wells-Barnett, *Crusade for Justice: The Autobiography of Ida B. Wells*, ed. Alfreda M. Duster (Chicago: The University of Chicago Press, 1970), chaps. 16, 29–32.

33. George W. Steevens, *The Land of the Dollar* (London: Wm. Blackwood & Sons, 1897), 144–52.

34. Isaac D. Rawlings et al., *The Rise and Fall of Disease in Illinois*, vol. 2 (Springfield, IL: Illinois Dept. of Public Health, 1927), table 1.

35. Hilda S. Polacheck, *I Came a Stranger: The Story of a Hull-House Girl* (Urbana: University of Illinois Press, 1989), 30.

36. Stead, *If Christ Came*, 187.

37. Lloyd Wendt and Herman Kogan, *Bosses in Lusty Chicago* (Bloomington: Indiana University Press, 1967), 111–35.

38. Wendt and Kogan, *Bosses*, 85–96, 282–90; Stead, *If Christ Came*, chap. 1.

39. Roy Rosenzweig, *Eight Hours for What We Will: Workers and Leisure in an Industrial City, 1870–1920* (New York: Cambridge University Press, 1983), chap. 2.

40. Lewis A. Erenberg, " 'Ain't We Got Fun?' " *Chicago History*, 14 (4): 4–21 (Winter 1985–86).

41. Nelson, *Beyond the Martyrs*, 18.

42. Kathleen D. McCarthy, *Noblesse Oblige: Charity and Cultural Philanthropy in Chicago, 1849–1929* (Chicago: The University of Chicago Press, 1982), chap. 5.

43. Stanley Buder, *Pullman: An Experiment in Industrial Order and Community Planning, 1880–1930* (New York: Oxford University Press, 1967), chaps. 1–4.

44. Wesley Skogan, *Chicago Since 1840: A Time-Series Data Handbook* (Urbana: University of Illinois Institute of Government and Public Affairs, 1976), table 2.

45. Helen Lefkowitz Horowitz, *Culture and the City: Cultural Philanthropy in Chicago from the 1880s to 1917* (Chicago: The University of Chicago Press, 1976), chap. 3.

46. Horowitz, *Culture and the City*, chap. 1.

47. Nelson, *Beyond the Martyrs*, chap. 1.

48. John B. Jentz, "Skilled Workers and Industrialization: Chicago's German Cabinetmakers and Machinists, 1880–1900," in Keil and Jentz, 73–85.

49. Indenture of William Lemme to Holmes, Pyott & Co., Chicago, April 23, 1902, Holmes & Pyott Collection, folder 2, Chicago Historical Society Archives and Manuscripts Dept.

50. Articles of Agreement, Architectural Iron Workers' Union and the Architectural Iron League, Chicago, June 19, 1899, Holmes & Pyott Collection, folder 2, Chicago Historical Society Archives and Manuscripts Dept.

51. James Barrett, "Immigrant Workers in Early Mass Production Industry: Work Rationalization and Job Control Conflicts in Chicago's Packinghouses, 1900–1904," in Keil and Jentz, 104–24.

52. Illinois Bureau of Labor Statistics, *First Report on Industrial Accidents in Illinois for the Six Months Ending December 31, 1907* (Springfield, IL: Phillips Bros., 1908), 19–21, 65–69.

53. Upton Sinclair, *The Jungle* (Urbana: University of Illinois Press, 1988 [orig. publ. 1906]), 76.

54. Theodore Dreiser, *Sister Carrie* (Philadelphia: University of Pennsylvania Press, 1981 [orig. publ. 1900]), 37–38.

55. United States Census Office, *Twelfth Census of the United States, 1900*, vol. 2 (Washington, DC: 1902), table 94, 558–60.

56. John Bogue, *Chicago Cheap Lodging Houses and Their Lodgers* (Chicago: Improved Housing Association of Chicago, 1899), passim.

57. Schedule of Prices, Demands of Local Unions No. 4 and No. 18, Chicago, 1905, Agnes Nestor Collection, box 1, folder 2, Chicago Historical Society Archives and Manuscripts Dept.

58. Agnes Nestor, Diary, entry of July 17, 1900, Chicago, Agnes Nestor Collection, box 1, folder 2, Chicago Historical Society Archives and Manuscripts Dept.

59. Form letter to the Manufacturers of the State of Illinois from the Illinois Association of Manufacturers, Chicago, March 15, 1895, Illinois Association of Manufacturers Collection, box 160, folder C, Chicago Historical Society Archives and Manuscripts Dept.

60. *Twelfth Census*, Population, vol. 2, table 94, 558–60.

61. David M. Katzman, *Seven Days a Week: Women and Domestic Service in Industrializing America* (New York: Oxford University Press, 1978), 71–79 and appendix 3.

62. Robert L. Reid, ed., *Battleground: The Autobiography of Margaret A. Haley* (Urbana: University of Illinois Press, 1982), chaps. 2 and 3.

63. *Second Annual Report of the Factory Inspectors of Illinois for the Year Ending December 15, 1894* (Springfield, IL: Edward F. Hartman, 1895), 13.

64. *Industrial School Songs*, South Side Tabernacle, Chicago, Shaw Wells Collection, box 1, folder 1, Chicago Historical Society Archives and Manuscripts Dept.

65. Letter from T. E. Daniels to the Manager, Libby Prison Museum, Feb. 20, 1890, Libby Prison Collection, folder 3, Chicago Historical Society Archives and Manuscripts Dept.

66. *Fourth Annual Report of the Factory Inspectors of Illinois for the Year Ending December 15, 1896* (Springfield, IL: Phillips Brothers, 1897), 17.

67. Broadside, *The Chicago Relief and Aid Society* (Chicago: engraving by Benedict & Co., 1896–1900), Chicago Historical Society Prints and Photographs Collection.

68. *Chicago Daily News Almanac for 1891*, comp. G. E. Plumbe (Chicago: The Chicago Daily News Co., 1891), 102.

69. Ginger, *Altgeld's America*, 92.

70. Stead, *If Christ Came*, 72–73.

71. Stead, *If Christ Came*, 465.

72. McCarthy, *Noblesse Oblige*, 68–70.

73. Ginger, *Altgeld's America*, 250; Civic Federation of Chicago, *Report of the Central Relief Association to the Civic Federation* (Chicago: Wm. C. Hollister & Bro., Printers, 1894), 19–20.

74. Jane Addams, *Twenty Years at Hull-House* (New York: New American Library, 1961), 127–32.

75. Nestor Diary, Nov. 12, 1900, Chicago Historical Society.

76. Buder, *Pullman*, chaps. 5–11.

77. Buder, *Pullman*, chaps. 12–15.

78. Almont Lindsey, *The Pullman Strike* (Chicago: The University of Chicago Press, 1942).

79. Letter of Bertha Palmer to Richard Easley, Aug. 11, 1894, World Columbian Exposition Collection, folder 17a, Chicago Historical Society Archives and Manuscripts Dept.

80. Nick Salvatore, *Eugene V. Debs: Citizen and Socialist* (Urbana: University of Illinois Press, 1982), part 2.

81. Jane Addams, "A Modern Lear," in Graham Taylor, *Satellite Cities* (New York: D. Appleton and Co., 1915), 68–90.

82. U.S. Strike Commission, *Report on the Chicago Strike of June-July 1894*, 53d Cong., 3d session, 1895 Ex Doc 7, XLVI–LIV.

Visions of a Better Chicago

1. *Chicago Tribune*, Aug. 8, 1889, 1, quoted in Mel Scott, *American City Planning* (Berkeley: University of California Press, 1971), 32.

2. "Chicago in the World's Fair Year," *Chicago Tribune*, Oct. 12, 1890, 12.

3. The close association of the fair and the urban redevelopment of Paris and its celebrated 1889 exposition are discussed in Russell Lewis, "Everything Under One Roof: World's Fairs and Department Stores in Paris and Chicago," *Chicago History* 12 (3): 35–47 (Fall 1983).

4. Quoted in R. Reid Badger, *The Great American Fair: The World's Columbian Exposition and American Culture* (Chicago: Nelson Hall, 1979), 96.

5. Lewis, "Everything Under One Roof," 41.

6. Harold Mayer and Richard Wade, *Chicago: Growth of a Metropolis* (Chicago: The University of Chicago Press, 1969), 140.

7. Seventeen (68%) of the 25 individuals and companies holding over $25,000 worth of shares in the fair were railways. Chicago City Railway Company and West Chicago Street Railway Company each held $100,000 of the fair's shares. *The Daily News Almanac and Political Register for 1891* (Chicago: Chicago Daily News), 85. Harold L. Platt notes that Samuel Insull installed a large Corliss engine at the fair as part of his publicity campaign to dominate Chicago's market; see "Sam Insull and the Electrification of Chicago, 1880–1925" (Paper presented to the Organization of American Historians, Philadelphia, April 1982). This paper is available at the library of the Chicago Historical Society.

8. John Ellis, ed., *Chicago and the World's Columbian Exposition* (Chicago: Trans-Continental Art Publishing Co., 1895), passim; J. P. Barrett, *Electricity at the World's Columbian Exposition* (Chicago: R. R. Donnelley & Sons, 1894), 6–25.

9. Barrett, *Electricity at the Columbian Exposition*, 403–5.

10. Columbian Movable Sidewalk Co., *The Movable Sidewalk or Multiple Speed Railway* (Chicago: 1893), 1–3.

11. Quoted in Barrett, *Electricity at the Columbian Exposition*, vii.

12. Russell Lynes, *The Lively Audience: A Social History of the Visual and Performing Arts in America, 1890–1950* (New York: Harper and Row, 1985), 54.

13. Mrs. Mark Stevens, *Six Months at the World's Fair* (Detroit: Detroit Free Press Company, 1895), quoted in Sisley Barnes, "George Ferris' Wheel: The Great Attraction of the Midway Plaisance," *Chicago History* 6 (3): 177 (Fall 1977).

14. Barnes, "George Ferris' Wheel," passim.

15. For a general discussion of this intersection of business and community life see Peter Dobkin Hall, *The Organization of American Culture* (New York: New York University Press, 1982), 240–81.

16. For a survey of private collecting in Chicago see Patricia Erens, *Masterworks: Famous Chicagoans and their Paintings* (Chicago: Chicago Review Press, 1979).

17. Kathleen D. McCarthy, *Noblesse Oblige: Charity and Cultural Philanthropy in Chicago, 1849–1929* (Chicago: The University of Chicago Press, 1982), 49–50.

18. Roy Rosenzweig, *Eight Hours for What We Will: Workers and Leisure in an Industrial City* (New York: Cambridge University Press, 1983), passim.

19. For a discussion of this building see Linda S. Phipps, "The 1893 Art Institute Building and the 'Paris of America': Aspirations of Patrons and Architects in Late Nineteenth-Century Chicago," *The Art Institute of Chicago Museum Studies* 14 (1): 28–45 (1988).

20. Frederic Cople Jaher, *The Urban Establishment: Upper Strata in Boston, New York, Charleston, Chicago, and Los Angeles* (Urbana: University of Illinois Press, 1982), 523–26.

21. Rose Fay Thomas to Frances Glessner, May 3, 1892 (typescript), Glessner Papers, Chicago Historical Society Archives and Manuscripts Dept.

22. Perry Duis, *Creating New Traditions* (Chicago: Chicago Historical Society, 1976), 80.

23. Duis, *Creating New Traditions*, 89–91; for a complete account of Thomas's life see Ezra Schabas, *Theodore Thomas: America's Conductor and Builder of Orchestras, 1835–1905* (Urbana: University of Illinois Press, 1989).

24. For a discussion of late nineteenth-century professionalism see John Higham, "The Construction of American History," in John Higham, ed., *The Reconstruction of American History* (New York: Harper & Row, 1962), 18–19.

25. For a discussion of the new anthropology see George W. Stocking, Jr., ed., *Malinowski, Rivers, Benedict and Others: Essays on Culture and Personality* (Madison: University of Wisconsin Press, 1986), 13–49.

26. Turner's speech, "The Significance of the Closing of the American Frontier," was subsequently published in the *American Historical Association Annual Report for 1893* (Washington, DC: Smithsonian Institution, 1894), 197–227.

27. Jaher, *The Urban Establishment*, 520–21.

28. Helen Lefkowitz Horowitz, *Culture in the City: Cultural Philanthropy in Chicago from the 1880s to 1917* (Lexington: The University Press of Kentucky, 1976), 104. For a general survey of this period see Richard J. Storr, *Harper's University: The Beginnings* (Chicago: The University of Chicago Press, 1966). A general discussion of the relationships between universities and their communities can be found in Edward Shils, "The University, the City, and the World: Chicago and the University of Chicago," in Thomas Bender, ed., *The University and the City: From Medieval Origins to the Present* (New York: Oxford University Press, 1988).

29. Duis, *Creating New Traditions*, 64, 77–78.

30. Chester Carney, "Truancy in the Tenement District of Chicago," 1905 typescript quoted in Perry Duis, *The Saloon* (Urbana: University of Illinois Press, 1983), 100. The term *materialism* is used in this essay to refer to the belief, existing from the ancient Greeks to Thomas Hobbes, that people often define their environment through its physical characteristics. Associations with the psychological and Marxist interpretations of the nineteenth and twentieth centuries are not intended.

31. *Harper's Weekly*, 1893, quoted in Michael Ebner, *Creating Chicago's North Shore* (Chicago: The University of Chicago Press, 1988), 49.

32. For a general discussion of Marshall Field's see Russell Lewis, "Everything Under One Roof," passim.

33. Ebner, *Creating Chicago's North Shore*, 43–49, 127–31.

34. Mayer and Wade, *Chicago*, 150–60.

35. Eric H. Monkkonen, *America Becomes Urban: The Development of U. S. Cities & Towns, 1780–1980* (Berkeley: University of California Press, 1988), 199.

36. Kenan Heise and Mark Fruzel, *Hands on Chicago: Getting Hold of the City* (Chicago: Bonus Books, Inc., 1987), 74; Perry R. Duis and Glen R. Holt, "Little Boxes, Big Fortunes," *Chicago* 26 (11): 114–18 (Nov. 1977); Gwendolyn Wright, *Moralism and the Model Home: Domestic Architecture and Cultural Conflict in Chicago, 1873–1913* (Chicago: The University of Chicago Press, 1980), 40–45.

37. For a discussion of public attitudes toward lighting, see Mark J. Bourman, " 'A Light is as Good as a Policeman': Police Aspects of the Demand for Street Lighting in Nineteenth-Century American Cities" (Paper delivered to the American Studies Association, New York, Nov. 23, 1987).

38. Harold Richard Vynne, *Chicago by Day and Night* (Chicago: Thomson and Zimmerman, 1892), 23, passim.

39. The Gunther collection was acquired by the Chicago Historical Society in 1920. For a general discussion of Gunther's museum see Clement M. Silvestro, "The Candy Man's Mixed Bag," *Chicago History* 2 (2): 86–99 (Fall 1972).

40. Perry R. Duis, "Cheap Thrills and Dime Museums," *Chicago* 26 (10): 104–8 (Oct. 1977).

41. Lewis A. Erenberg, *Steppin' Out: New York Nightlife and the Transformation of American Culture, 1890–1930* (Chicago: The University of Chicago Press, 1981), 17–20; see also Erenberg, " 'Ain't We Got Fun?' " *Chicago History*, 14 (4): 4–21 (Winter 1985–86).

42. John L. Scherer, *Music Hall to Movie Palaces* (Hamilton, NY: Gallery Association of New York State, 1985), 12–19.

43. Miles Orvell, *The Real Thing: Imitation and Authenticity in American Culture, 1880–1940* (Chapel Hill: The University of North Carolina Press, 1989), 141–56.

44. Rosenzweig, *Eight Hours for What We Will*, passim.

45. For discussions of courtship see Ellen K. Rothman, *Hands and Hearts: A History of Courtship in America*, rev. ed. (Cambridge, MA: Harvard University Press, 1987) and Steven Mintz and Susan M. Kellogg, *Domestic Revolutions: A Social History of American Family Life* (Boston: Free Press, 1987).

46. For a discussion of limited privacy see Kathy Peiss, *Cheap Amusements: Working Women and Leisure in Turn-of-the-Century New York* (Philadelphia: Temple University Press, 1986), chap. 2.

47. Harvey Green, *Fit for America: Health, Fitness, Sport and American Society* (Baltimore, MD: Johns Hopkins University Press, 1986), 228–33.

48. Editor's remarks, *Wheel Talk*, 1 (6). This periodical was published in Chicago in 1895.

49. For an account of one such club see "Looking Backward: Around Town with the Saddle and Cycle Club," *Chicago History* 11 (2): 112–13 (Summer 1982).

50. George Bushnell, "When Chicago Was Wheel Crazy," *Chicago History* 4 (3): 167–75 (Fall 1975).

51. T. A. Faulkner, *From the Ball Room to Hell* (Chicago: Henry Bros. & Co., 1894).

52. Faulkner, *From the Ball Room to Hell*, 14–15.

53. *Souvenir of the Cake Walk* (Chicago: F. W. Bruckle, 1898).

54. Erenberg, " 'Ain't We Got Fun?' " 14–15. For a general discussion see Duis, *Creating New Traditions*, 91–96, Kalton C. Lahue, ed., *Motion Picture Pioneer: The Selig Polyscope Company* (Cranbury, NJ: A. S. Barnes & Co., 1973), and Charles A. Jahant, "Chicago: Center of the Silent Film Industry," *Chicago History*, 3 (1): 45–53 (Spring–Summer 1974).

55. See Jane Addams, *Twenty Years at Hull-House* (New York: New American Library, 1961), 75–100, passim.

56. McCarthy, *Noblesse Oblige*, 109.

57. *Hull-House Bulletin*, 1 (Chicago: 1895).

58. Chicago and Alton Railroad Co., *A Guide to the Chicago Drainage Canal* (Chicago: 1895), 3. For a general discussion see Louis P. Cain, "The Creation of Chicago's Sanitary District and Construction of the Sanitary and Ship Canal," *Chicago History* 8 (2): 98–110 (Summer 1979), and Louis P. Cain, *Sanitation Strategy for a Lakefront Metropolis: The Case of Chicago* (Chicago: Public Works History Association, 1978).

59. B. A. Eckhart to General R. A. Alger, March 31, 1900, Russell A. Alger Collection, Chicago Historical Society Archives and Manuscripts Dept. For a review of this approach to water treatment see Joel A. Tarr et al., "Water and Wastes: A Retrospective Assessment of Wastewater Technology in the United States, 1800–1932," *Technology and Culture* 25: 226–63 (1984).

60. William Thomas Stead, *If Christ Came to Chicago* (Chicago: Laird and Lee, 1894), 187.

61. Charles Zueblin, "Municipal Playgrounds in Chicago," *The American Journal of Sociology* 4: 145–58 (Sept. 1898).

62. "Want Sunlight in Slums," *Chicago Tribune*, Nov. 12, 1899, 2.

63. For a general discussion of the playground movement see Michael McCarthy, "Businessmen and Professionals in Municipal Reform: The Chicago Experience, 1887–1920," (Ph.D. diss., Northwestern University, 1970), chap. 3.

64. "Breaths of Summer," in Chicago Commons Association, *Chicago Commons—A Social Settlement* (Chicago: P. F. Pettibone & Co., 1899), 23–24.

65. For a discussion of this development see Anthony M. Platt, *The Child Savers: The Invention of Delinquency* (Chicago: The University of Chicago Press, 1969), 123–36, passim; Duis, *Creating New Traditions*, 70.

66. Albion Small to Jane Addams, Chicago, Dec. 26, 1893, Civic Federation of Chicago Papers, Chicago Historical Society Archives and Manuscripts Dept.

67. For a general discussion of the League see Sidney I. Roberts, "The Municipal Voters' League and Chicago's Boodlers," *Journal of the Illinois State Historical Society* 63: 117–48 (1960).

68. George Cole to Joseph Downey, March 6, 1896, Municipal Voters' League Papers, Chicago Historical Society Archives and Manuscripts Dept.

69. Quoted in Ray Ginger, *Altgeld's America: Chicago from 1892–1905* (New York: Markus Wiener Publishing Inc., 1986; reprint of 1958 edition), 256.

70. Mayer and Wade, *Chicago*, 140–42.

71. Ginger, *Altgeld's America*, 180–82.

72. These efforts proved unsuccessful; for a discussion see Maureen A. Flanagan, "Charter Reform in Chicago: Political Culture and Urban Progressive Reform," *Journal of Urban History* 12: 109–30 (1986).

73. Scott, *American City Planning*, 10–11.

74. For a more general discussion see *A Breath of Fresh Air: Chicago's Neighborhood Parks of the Progressive Reform Era, 1900–1925* (Chicago: Chicago Public Library, 1989).

Afterword

1. Douglas S. Massey, "Segregation and the Underclass in Chicago," *Chicago Community Trust Human Relations Task Force: A Report on Race, Ethnic, & Religious Tensions in Chicago* (Chicago: Sept. 1989), 108.

2. *Chicago Tribune*, Nov. 7, 1987, 1, 1:2.

Bibliographic Essay

This essay focuses on secondary publications and is intended to provide access to further information and discussion of the topics touched upon in this publication. Specific references for primary and unpublished materials can be located in notes that accompany the essays in this publication.

Theodore Dreiser's *Sister Carrie* (Philadelphia: University of Pennsylvania Press, 1981 [orig. publ. 1900]) is both an American literary classic and an excellent introduction to the dreams and experiences of a young newcomer to Chicago in the 1890s. Ray Ginger's *Altgeld's America: The Lincoln Ideal versus Changing Realities* (New York: Markus Wiener Publishing, Inc., 1986) provides a good overview of many aspects of life in Chicago in the 1890s as it explores the career and causes of John Peter Altgeld.

Melvin Holli and Peter d'A. Jones, eds., *Ethnic Chicago*, rev. ed. (Grand Rapids, MI: William B. Eerdmans Publishing Co., 1984) is a good introduction to the wide range of Chicago's ethnic and racial groups. Some studies of specific groups and autobiographies also cover the 1890s: Ira Berkow, *Maxwell Street: Survival in a Bazaar* (Garden City, NY: Doubleday & Co., Inc., 1977); Odd S. Lovoll, *A Century of Urban Life: The Norwegians in Chicago before 1930* (Northfield, MN: Norwegian-American Historical Association, 1988); Lawrence J. McCaffrey, et al., *The Irish in Chicago* (Urbana: University of Illinois Press, 1987); Humbert S. Nelli, *The Italians in Chicago, 1880–1930* (New York: Oxford University Press, 1970); Hilda S. Polacheck, *I Came a Stranger: The Story of a Hull-House Girl* (Urbana:

University of Illinois Press, 1989); Allan Spear, *Black Chicago: The Making of a Negro Ghetto, 1890–1920* (Chicago: The University of Chicago Press, 1967). No historian, however, has written a comprehensive work on the major group of the 1890s, the Germans.

Although Germans as an ethnic group have not had their historians, the German working class has. The results of a large study initiated at the University of Munich are collected in Hartmut Keil and John B. Jentz, eds., *German Workers in Industrial Chicago, 1850–1910: A Comparative Perspective* (DeKalb: Northern Illinois University Press, 1983). Bruce Nelson, *Beyond the Martyrs: A Social History of Chicago's Anarchists, 1870–1900* (New Brunswick, NJ: Rutgers University Press, 1988), explores the predominantly German radical movement in Chicago and also gives an excellent analysis of industrial development and the changing nature of work in the city. A classic source for the lives of the immigrant poor in the meat-packing industry is Upton Sinclair, *The Jungle* (Urbana: University of Illinois Press, 1988 [orig. publ. 1906]).

Stanley Buder explores the model town of Pullman in *Pullman: An Experiment in Industrial Order and Community Planning, 1880–1930* (New York: Oxford University Press, 1967). The local and national aspects of the Pullman Strike are explored by Almont Lindsey in *The Pullman Strike* (Chicago: The University of Chicago Press, 1942).

The problems of the poor, vice, and corrupt politics as well as some solutions to them are best explored in two books of the time:

William T. Stead, *If Christ Came to Chicago* (Chicago: Laird & Lee, 1894) and Jane Addams, *Twenty Years at Hull-House* (New York: New American Library, 1961 [orig. publ., 1910]). More specialized studies are: Perry R. Duis, *The Saloon: Public Drinking in Chicago and Boston, 1880–1920* (Urbana: University of Illinois Press, 1983); and Lloyd Wendt and Herman Kogan, *Bosses in Lusty Chicago* (Bloomington: Indiana University Press, 1967).

The most accessible general survey of the World's Columbian Exposition of 1893, including its construction and the accompanying World Congresses, is R. Reid Badger's *The Great American Fair: The World's Columbian Exposition and American Culture* (Chicago: Nelson-Hall, 1979). Stanley Appelbaum, *The Chicago World's Fair of 1893: A Photographic Record* (New York: Dover, 1980) provides an intriguing visual survey of the fairgrounds and related activities. A recent addition to the literature on the significance of the fair can be found in Ross Miller's *American Apocalypse: The Great Fire and the Myth of Chicago* (Chicago: The University of Chicago Press, 1990).

The concept of private contributions to a city has been explored in Sam Bass Warner, Jr., *The Private City: Philadelphia in Three Periods of its Growth* (Philadelphia: University of Pennsylvania Press, 1968). Private philanthropy and its influence on Chicago's development has received significant attention in recent years. Three major studies on the wealthy residents of late nineteenth-century Chicago are Frederick Cople Jaher, *The Urban Establishment* (Urbana: University of Illinois Press, 1982); Helen Lefkowitz Horowitz, *Culture and the City: Cultural Philanthropy in Chicago from the 1880s to 1917* (Lexington: The University Press of Kentucky, 1976); and Kathleen D. McCarthy, *Noblesse Oblige: Charity and Cultural Philanthropy in Chicago, 1849–1929* (Chicago: The University of Chicago Press, 1982). Each of these discusses the relationship between this group and the cultural activities of the city.

A useful introduction to the collections of the Art Institute is John Maxon, *The Art Institute of Chicago* (New York: Thames and Hudson, Ltd., 1970); studies of specific historical aspects can be found in *The Art Institute of Chicago Museum Studies* (1974–). The formation and early years of the Chicago Orchestra is the subject of Philo Adams Otis, *The Chicago Symphony Orchestra* (Chicago: Clayton F. Summy Co., 1925) and its founder is treated in Ezra Schabas, *Theodore Thomas: America's Conductor and Builder of Orchestras, 1835–1905* (Urbana: University of Illinois Press, 1989). The collections of the Field Museum are briefly outlined in *General Guide to The Field Museum of Natural History* (Chicago: Field Museum of Natural History, 1971). Among the many publications on the early years of The University of Chicago are Richard J. Storr, *Harper's University: The Beginnings* (Chicago: The University of Chicago Press, 1966) and Jean F. Block, *The Uses of Gothic: Planning and Building the Campus of the University of Chicago, 1892–1932* (Chicago: University of Chicago Library, 1983).

Chicago has been recognized as an important national center of commerce, and specific investigations of materialism in the city focus on department stores and the development of mail-order businesses. Marshall Field's is the subject of two excellent publications: Robert W. Twyman, *History of Marshall Field & Co., 1852–1906* (Philadelphia: University of Pennsylvania Press, 1954) and Lloyd Wendt and Herman Kogan, *Give the Lady What She Wants! The Story of Marshall Field & Co.* (Chicago: Rand McNally, 1952). Additional studies on consumerism in Chicago include Boris Emmet and John Jeuck, *Catalogues and Counters: A History of Sears, Roebuck, & Company* (Chicago: The University of Chicago Press, 1950) and Joseph Siry's *Carson Pirie Scott: Louis Sullivan and the Chicago Department Store* (Chicago: The University of Chicago Press, 1988).

Relevant studies on the development of the new culture of youth can be found in several studies of this phenomenon; however, a single study on Chicago remains to be written. Joanne Meyerowitz examines the experiences of young women in *Women Adrift: Independent Wage Earners in Chicago, 1880–1930* (Chicago: The University of Chicago Press, 1988). Lewis Erenberg discusses the changing social scene of the period in *Steppin' Out: New York Nightlife and the Transformation of American Culture, 1890–1930* (Chicago: The University of Chicago Press, 1981). The development of bicycling and physical fitness are discussed by Harvey Green in *Fit for America: Health, Fitness, Sport and American Society* (Baltimore: Johns Hopkins University Press, 1986), and shifting national sexual attitudes are the subject of John D'Emilio and Estelle Freedman's *Intimate Matters: A History of Sexuality in America* (New York: Harper and Row, 1988).

The development of civic consciousness has been closely tied to the Progressive Era, and most relevant publications extend well into the twentieth century. There are biographies for many of the reformers involved in the settlement houses including Jane Addams, Florence Kelley, Julia Lathrop, and Mary McDowell. The interconnections of reformers in the multifaceted activities at the turn of the century are described by Louise Wade in *Graham Taylor: Pioneer for Social Justice, 1851–1938* (Chicago: The University of Chicago Press, 1964), and the development of the juvenile court has been traced by Anthony M. Platt in *The Child Savers: The Invention of Delinquency* (Chicago: The University of Chicago Press, 1969). The early efforts of the Civic Federation have been chronicled in *Fifty Years at the Civic Front, 1893–1943* (Chicago: The Civic Federation, 1943). The Municipal Voters' League is the subject of an extended study by Sidney Roberts in "The Municipal Voters' League and Chicago's Boodlers," *Journal of the Illinois State Historical Society* 53 (1960): 117–48. The emergence of the playground movement in Chicago is the subject of Dominick Cavallo's *Muscles and Morals: Organized Playgrounds and Urban Reform, 1880–1920* (Philadelphia: University of Pennsylvania Press, 1981). A full biography of Charles Yerkes and the battle over the streetcar franchise has yet to be published; however, Yerkes is the subject of fictional accounts by Edgar Lee Masters in *The Tale of Chicago* (1933) and by Theodore Dreiser in *The Financier* (1912), *The Stoic* (1947), and *The Titan* (1914).

Illustrations

69 right, CHS Archives and Manuscripts Dept.; 70 above, CHS Archives and Manuscripts Dept.; 70 below, from *The Graphic* (June 17, 1893), CHS Library; 71, CHS Prints and Photographs Collection; 72, from *If Christ Came to Chicago* (1894), CHS Library; 73, from "Central Relief Association" (1894), CHS Library; 74 above, University of Illinois at Chicago, the University Library, Jane Addams Memorial Collection; 74 below, CHS, ICHi-21774; 75 above, CHS Prints and Photographs Collection; 75 below, CHS Library; 76, CHS, ICHi-21031; 77 above, CHS, G1982.157 #P63316; 77 below, CHS Archives and Manuscripts Dept.; 78 above, CHS, ICHi-09990; 78 below, CHS, ICHi-04908; 79, CHS, ICHi-01922; 80, CHS Decorative and Industrial Arts Collection; 81 above left, from *Harper's Weekly* (July 21, 1894), CHS Library; 81 below left, CHS Archives and Manuscripts Dept.; 81 bottom, CHS Costumes Collection; 82, CHS Library.

Color Plates
83, CHS Library; 84, CHS Prints and Photographs Collection; 85 above, CHS, ICHi-21844; 85 below left and below right, CHS Decorative and Industrial Arts Collection; 86, CHS Prints and Photographs Collection; 87, CHS Prints and Photographs Collection; 88, CHS Prints and Photographs Collection; 89 above, CHS Architectural Collection; 89 below, CHS Decorative and Industrial Arts Collection.

Visions of a Better Chicago
90, CHS Paintings and Sculpture Collection; 91, CHS, ICHi-02520; 92, CHS, ICHi-02524; 93, CHS, ICHi-02543; 94, CHS Decorative and Industrial Arts Collection; 95, Irish-American Heritage Center; 96, CHS Library; 97, CHS Library; 98, CHS Prints and Photographs Collection; 99, CHS Paintings and Sculpture Collection; 100 above, CHS Decorative and Industrial Arts Collection; 100 below, CHS, ICHi-13686; 101 above, CHS Library; 101 below, CHS Decorative and Industrial Arts Collection; 102 above, CHS Library; 102 below, CHS Decorative and Industrial Arts Collection; 103, CHS Prints and Photographs Collection; 104, CHS, ICHi-17426; 105, CHS Prints and Photographs Collection; 106 left, CHS, ICHi-16827; 106 right, CHS Prints and Photographs Collection; 107 left, CHS Prints and Photographs Collection; 107 right, CHS, ICHi-09424; 108 above, CHS, ICHi-19219; 108 below, CHS, ICHi-10791; 109 above, CHS, ICHi-20431; 109 below, Installation of the European Paintings galleries at the Art Institute of Chicago, c. 1900. (©1990 The Art Institute of Chicago, all rights reserved); 110, CHS Prints and Photographs Collection; 111 above, CHS, ICHi-21969; 111 below, CHS Prints and Photographs Collection, courtesy of the Chicago Symphony Orchestra; 112 above, CHS, ICHi-20386; 112 below left, CHS Library; 112 below right, gloves, top hat, and opera glasses, CHS Costumes Collection;

programs, CHS Library; 113, CHS, ICHi-02228; 114, Field Museum of Natural History (Neg# 8191), Chicago; 115, Field Museum of Natural History (Neg# 8407), Chicago; 116 above, University of Chicago Archives; 116 below, from *Cap and Gown '95* (1895), CHS Library; 117 above left, CHS, ICHi-19092; 117 above right, from Richard J. Storr, *Harper's University: The Beginnings*, The University of Chicago Press, 1966, photograph by Barnes-Crosby (©1966 by the University of Chicago, all rights reserved); 117 below, The University of Chicago; 118, CHS, ICHi-19071; 119 above, CHS Costumes Collection; 119 below, CHS, ICHi-20239; 120 above, middle, and right, CHS Costumes Collection; 120 below right, Marshall Field's Archives; 121 left, CHS, ICHi-21928; 121 above right and below right, CHS Costumes Collection; 122 left, CHS Decorative and Industrial Arts Collection; 122 right, CHS Prints and Photographs Collection; 123 left, CHS Prints and Photographs Collection; 123 right, tennis racket, CHS Decorative and Industrial Arts Collection; football and baseball, University of Chicago Athletic Dept.; 124, CHS, ICHi-20827; 125, Swedish American Museum Association of Chicago; 126, CHS, ICHi-06577; 127 left and middle, from *Tenth Annual Illustrated Catalog of S. E. Gross' Famous City Subdivisions and Suburban Towns* (1891), CHS Library; 127 right, CHS Library; 128 left, CHS Decorative and Industrial Arts Collection; 128 right, from "People's Outfitting Co. Catalog" (1891), CHS Library; 129 above, CHS, ICHi-21971; 129 below, CHS Prints and Photographs Collection; 130, CHS, ICHi-14494; 131 above, CHS Library; 131 below, CHS Library; 132, CHS, ICHi-21980; 133, CHS Library; 134 left, CHS Costumes Collection; 134 above and below, Schwinn History Center; 135, CHS, Prints and Photographs Collection; 136 left, CHS Prints and Photographs Collection; 136 right, from "Monarch Bicycle Co. Catalogue" (1897), CHS Library; 137 above, CHS Library; 137 below, Mr. and Mrs. Richard Powell; 138 above, CHS Library; 138 below, CHS Costumes Collection; 139 above, CHS Prints and Photographs Collection; 139 below, CHS, ICHi-19147; 140, CHS Decorative and Industrial Arts Collection; 141, CHS, ICHi-19288; 142 above, CHS, ICHi-21783; 142 below, University of Illinois at Chicago, the University Library, Jane Addams Memorial Collection; 144, CHS Decorative and Industrial Arts Collection; 145 above, from *A Guide to the Chicago Drainage Canal* (1895), CHS Library; 145 below left, CHS, ICHi-14865; 145 below right, CHS Decorative and Industrial Arts Collection; 146 above and below, University of Illinois at Chicago, the University Library, Jane Addams Memorial Collection; 147 above, CHS, ICHi-17104; 147 below, Chicago Park District; 148, CHS, ICHi-21994; 149 above, CHS, ICHi-21394; 149 below, CHS, ICHi-21367; 150 above, CHS, ICHi-13104; 150 below, from *The Graphic* (Jan. 22, 1898), CHS Library; 151, CHS, ICHi-21806; 152 above and below, CHS Architectural Collection.

Index

Illustrations are indicated in italics. If a subject is illustrated and discussed on the same page, the illustration is not separately indicated.